D0514030

vid
opperfield

Charles Dickens

Notes by Bernard Haughey

Longman   York Press

The right of Bernard Haughey to be identified as Author of this Work has been asserted by him in accordance with the Copyright, Designs and Patents Act 1988

YORK PRESS
322 Old Brompton Road, London SW5 9JH

Pearson Education Limited
Edinburgh Gate, Harlow,
Essex CM20 2JE, United Kingdom
Associated companies, branches and representatives throughout the world

© Librairie du Liban *Publishers* and Addison Wesley Longman Limited 1998

First published 1998
Second impression 1999

ISBN 0-582-36824-3

Designed by Vicki Pacey, Trojan Horse, London
Illustrated by William Geldart
Map by Neil Gower
Phototypeset by Gem Graphics, Trenance, Mawgan Porth, Cornwall
Colour reproduction and film output by Spectrum Colour
Produced by Addison Wesley Longman China Limited, Hong Kong

CONTENTS

PREFACE

York Notes are designed to give you a broader perspective on works of literature studied at GCSE and equivalent levels. We have carried out extensive research into the needs of the modern literature student prior to publishing this new edition. Our research showed that no existing series fully met students' requirements. Rather than present a single authoritative approach, we have provided alternative viewpoints, empowering students to reach their own interpretations of the text. York Notes provide a close examination of the work and include biographical and historical background, summaries, glossaries, analyses of characters, themes, structure and language, cultural connections and literary terms.

If you look at the Contents page you will see the structure for the series. However, there's no need to read from the beginning to the end as you would with a novel, play, poem or short story. Use the Notes in the way that suits you. Our aim is to help you with your understanding of the work, not to dictate how you should learn.

York Notes are written by English teachers and examiners, with an expert knowledge of the subject. They show you how to succeed in coursework and examination assignments, guiding you through the text and offering practical advice. Questions and comments will extend, test and reinforce your knowledge. Attractive colour design and illustrations improve clarity and understanding, making these Notes easy to use and handy for quick reference.

York Notes are ideal for:
- Essay writing
- Exam preparation
- Class discussion

The author of these Notes is Bernard Haughey, BA, a former Head of English who has taught in a variety of Technical Colleges, Grammar Schools and Comprehensive Schools and has been Head of English at St Gregory's Grammar School and The Barlow High School in Manchester. He has also worked as an English examiner for a major examination board.

The text used in these Notes is the Penguin Classics edition, with an introduction and notes by Jeremy Tambling, published in 1996.

Health Warning: **This study guide will enhance your understanding, but should not replace the reading of the original text and/or study in class.**

PART ONE

INTRODUCTION

HOW TO STUDY A NOVEL

You have bought this book because you wanted to study a novel on your own. This may supplement classwork.

- You will need to read the novel several times. Start by reading it quickly for pleasure, then read it slowly and carefully. Further readings will generate new ideas and help you to memorise the details of the story.
- Make careful notes on themes, plot and characters of the novel. The plot will change some of the characters. Who changes?
- The novel may not present events chronologically. Does the novel you are reading begin at the beginning of the story or does it contain flashbacks and a muddled time sequence? Can you think why?
- How is the story told? Is it narrated by one of the characters or by an all-seeing ('omniscient') narrator?
- Does the same person tell the story all the way through? Or do we see the events through the minds and feelings of a number of different people?
- Which characters does the narrator like? Which characters do you like or dislike? Do your sympathies change during the course of the book? Why? When?
- Any piece of writing (including your notes and essays) is the result of thousands of choices. No book had to be written in just one way: the author could have chosen other words, other phrases, other characters, other events. How could the author of your novel have written the story differently? If events were recounted by a minor character how would this change the novel?

Studying on your own requires self-discipline and a carefully thought-out work plan in order to be effective. Good luck.

Charles Dickens was born near Portsmouth on 7 February 1812, the second of eight children. His early childhood was spent at Portsmouth, where his father, John, worked as a clerk in the Navy Pay Office. His father's work necessitated moving from place to place, and the family lived also at Chatham and in London.

The family was always financially insecure and Charles's father, together with all the family except Charles, was imprisoned for debt in the Marshalsea Debtors' Prison. Charles was set to work in Warren's Blacking Warehouse, near Charing Cross, at six shillings a week. He felt deep shame at his menial job and his family's misfortune.

Upon receipt of a legacy, his father was released from prison and Charles was sent to school, where he proved a successful pupil. In 1827, he was articled to a firm of solicitors at Gray's Inn. He taught himself shorthand, worked as a freelance reporter and began to report parliamentary debates.

His relationships with women were not easy. He fell passionately in love with Maria Beadnell, but his love was unrequited. He was unkind to his wife, Catherine, who bore him ten children and left him after twenty-two years. His relationship with his children was unhappy too. His last love was Ellen Ternan, an actress.

When Charles was twenty-one, his *Sketches by Boz* was published in *The Monthly Magazine*, and in 1834 he became a reporter on the *Morning Chronicle*. He was commissioned to write a monthly series and *Pickwick Papers* was born.

As editor of *Bentley's Miscellany*, Dickens published *Oliver Twist* (1837) under the pseudonym of Boz, again in serial form. The evil consequences of the Poor Law of 1834 and the harshness of life in the workhouse are dramatically exposed in this novel.

Nicholas Nickleby (1838–9) attacks the unjust and cruel treatment of children in some educational establishments. We trace an echo of this in the Salem House of Creakle and Tungay in *David Copperfield* (1849–50), where we also encounter corruption in the legal system (dealt with again in *Bleak House* (1852–3)) and the desperate state of the poor (a theme of *Hard Times* (1854)).

Charles fought for social justice, as a campaigner as well as a writer, and felt deeply the injustices inflicted upon the poor by the penal system and its upholders.

By 1865, he had produced fourteen major works, which established him as a writer of world renown and as one of the most popular English novelists. Many of his larger-than-life characters are as famous today as ever.

Readers of *David Copperfield* will easily note certain parallels between the novel and Dickens's own life. Dickens sees David as himself. This is, no doubt, why he admitted that, of all his works, *David Copperfield* was the novel he himself most enjoyed.

The pressure of his writing and the exhausting public readings of his works, together with his many other interests, eventually damaged his health, and he died of a stroke on 9 June 1870. He is buried in Poets' Corner in Westminster Abbey.

CONTEXT & SETTING

The Industrial Revolution In the nineteenth century there was a massive movement of population from the countryside to the industrial towns to find work in the mills, factories and mines. This movement was accompanied by an

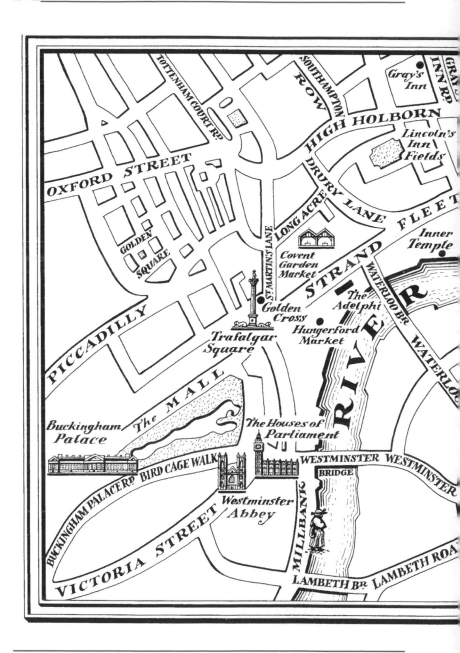

enormous rise in population. The poor were crowded into unsuitable housing in insanitary conditions and lived in great squalor. At one stage 20,000 people were living in cellars in Manchester alone.

Though Britain was the largest manufacturing power in the world, the poor did not share in the national prosperity. The middle-class industrialists became rich and their political power increased, but there was a threat of revolution from the impoverished working class, who had no political power at all. There were indeed two nations.

After the Napoleonic War ended in 1815, unemployment was high and cheap imported corn meant losses for British landowners. The Corn Laws were introduced to protect the price of British corn and the cost of bread doubled, while wages remained the same. There were riots by the starving poor.

The poor were punished severely by the law.

Landowners enclosed woods to prevent people catching game for food, and poachers could be hanged. Even owning nets for catching rabbits held a penalty of transportation to Australia for seven years.

Mill owners operated a 'truck' system, whereby part of the labourer's wage was paid in vouchers which could be used to buy goods only in the mill owner's shop. Income tax, which the rich alone paid, was abolished and indirect taxation, which hit the poor more than the rich, was increased.

The Poor Law Amendment Act of 1834, though well-intentioned, in practice deprived thousands of poor people of the outdoor relief, their only means of support, and drove them to the workhouses, where conditions were very harsh (see *Oliver Twist*).

People were harder to control in the towns. The extended families of village life had been broken up and the father as the sole authoritarian head of the family became the norm. It is not surprising that the rich went in fear of the poor, some of whom were intent on revolution rather than reform, and all of whom were simmering with discontent.

The 1816 Habeas Corpus Act meant that for civil offences people could be kept in custody without charge and the Six Acts of 1819 allowed magistrates to search houses without warrants and to try people without judge and jury. Large gatherings were banned and stamp duty was increased on pamphlets and periodicals, making it more difficult for the less well-off to campaign for their cause in print. Massacres of civilians at Peterloo in 1819, and at Newport in 1839 bore witness to the severity of the repression.

Help for the poor

There were some positive signs, however. The Reform Bill (1832) allowed workers to form unions though with restrictions which ensured the unions were weak. Previously (1824), six farmworkers from Tolpuddle in Dorset had been punished for forming a union.

Another improvement was the cheap postage system (1840), which enabled workers to communicate with one another nation-wide. The repeal of the Corn Laws (1846) brought some relief to the poor. Industrialists were against the Corn Laws and their passing showed how power was being transferred from the landed gentry to the middle classes. The Factory Act (1819) was an attempt to improve the lot of children in industry. Children under nine were forbidden to be employed in mills and nine- to sixteen-year-olds were limited to twelve hours' work a day.

The Gaol Act of 1823 abolished some of the worst abuses in prisons. Magistrates were committed to inspect prisons three times a quarter. Other improvements were: elementary education for prisoners; visits from doctors and clergymen; women warders for women prisoners, and a paid staff of warders.

Inadequate elementary education

Education in the country at large was sparse before 1870. There were numbers of voluntary schools, some run by the churches, but at the time of Dickens's birth, only one in seventeen of the working class received any elementary education at all.

The railways opened up the country and, though initially they were meant for the transport of goods and materials, eventually they transported people as well at a rate of a penny a mile. This enabled the middle class to move out of the overcrowded and unhealthy towns into the suburbs. Paradoxically, this meant worse slums for the poor in towns.

An age of great literature

The nineteenth century saw the rise of some of our greatest novelists, such as the Brontës, George Eliot, Anthony Trollope, W.M. Thackeray and Thomas Hardy; poets such as Robert Browning, Gerard Manley Hopkins, A.E. Housman, Charles Algernon Swinburne, the Pre-Raphaelites and Rudyard Kipling. There were also many writers of renown in other fields like philosophy and the world of politics.

On the one hand, it was an age of wonderful inventiveness and staggering development, while on the other, it was a time when many led lives of abject misery and the immense growth of wealth among the few oppressed, rather than aided, the impoverished majority.

Dickens's characters reflecting their times.

It was an era when those in authority forced their will brutally on those in their charge, a reflection of which we can see in the bullying tactics of the Murdstones and Creakle.

The Micawbers are certainly victims of the condition

applying to their times, when people could be gaoled for not being able to pay their way. David's treatment on the road to Dover, as he is running away to Betsey's, shows the links between crime and poverty with the poor preying upon the poor. The appalling conditions at Murdstone and Grinby's warehouse to which David was subjected give us an insight into the working conditions of the time and the despair that they engendered.

We can observe, therefore, in *David Copperfield* much of the spirit of the times in which it was written and experience, through Dickens's characters, the effect it had on the people.

PART TWO

Summaries

General summary

PART 1

*Chapters 1–18
(Childhood and
education)*

When David is born, his mother, Clara, is already a widow. His Aunt Betsey is annoyed that the baby is not a girl and leaves abruptly. David's nurse, Peggotty, looks after him and his young mother.

Peggotty takes David for a holiday to her brother Dan's house, a beached boat, at Yarmouth, where Dan cares for two orphans, Ham and Emily, and a widow, Mrs Gummidge. David is very happy there and feels he is in love with Emily.

On his return home, he discovers his mother has married the severe Mr Murdstone, whose aim it is to discipline Clara and David in 'firmness' of character. His equally daunting sister and ally, Miss Murdstone, comes to live with them, and David and his mother are cruelly treated. While being thrashed by Mr Murdstone, David bites his stepfather's hand and is sent away to the infamous Mr Creakle's Salem House school. Here David makes friends with Steerforth, a privileged pupil, and Thomas Traddles.

Upon the tragic death of his mother and baby brother, David is removed from school. Peggotty is sacked and returns home to her brother, taking David with her for a holiday. During David's stay at Yarmouth, Peggotty marries Barkis, the carrier.

Mr Murdstone puts David to work in appalling conditions in his wine business. David lodges with Mr Micawber, who is eventually imprisoned for debt. Freed from prison, Mr Micawber leaves London and David resolves to run away to look for his Aunt Betsey in Dover. After a harrowing journey, David arrives at his aunt's and is taken into her household, which includes a Mr Dick.

Betsey goes for advice on David's schooling to Mr Wickfield, at whose house in Canterbury David meets his clerk, Uriah Heep. David lodges with Mr Wickfield and his young daughter, Agnes, while attending Dr Strong's school, where he is very happy and successful. Dr Strong helps his wife's cousin, Jack Maldon, to emigrate to India. On the night of his departure, Maldon seriously upsets Strong's wife, Annie. Mr Dick keeps in contact with David and becomes friendly with the Strongs. He tells David about a strange man lurking around Betsey's house and frightening her.

PART *2*

Chapters 19–30 (Steerforth again; Dora)

After leaving school, David visits London and Suffolk on his own. First he sees Agnes and Mr Wickfield, who is in poor health. In London David meets Steerforth again and visits his home, where he gets to know Rosa Dartle, Mrs Steerforth and Littimer, Steerforth's servant.

David invites Steerforth to Mr Peggotty's. They arrive just as Ham announces his engagement to Emily.

David is to enter the law firm of Spenlow and Jorkins at Aunt Betsey's expense. He takes rooms at Mrs Crupp's. Agnes warns David about Steerforth and announces that Heep is going into partnership with Mr Wickfield, whom he is controlling. Heep admits having designs on Agnes.

Mr Spenlow introduces David to his daughter, Dora, and he is immediately infatuated. He meets again Miss Murdstone who is Dora's companion. David meets his old schoolfriend, Traddles, who lodges with the Micawbers and is engaged to Sophy. On Steerforth's return from Yarmouth, he tries to delay David's visit to Peggotty whose husband is ill. His illness and death have delayed Emily's marriage to

Ham. David finds her behaving oddly, perhaps affected by Barkis's death.

PART 3

Chapters 31–38 (Emily lost; David and Dora)

In great distress, Ham informs the family that Emily has eloped with Steerforth and offers all his money to Mr Peggotty to assist him in his search for Emily.

Aunt Betsey is ruined and has to live with David at Mrs Crupp's. Heep and his mother now live at Mr Wickfield's. David takes a post as part-time secretary to Dr Strong and, in order to pursue a career as a parliamentary reporter, teaches himself shorthand. Traddles finds work for Mr Dick, and Mr Micawber is employed as Heep's clerk.

Miss Murdstone discloses David's love letters to Mr Spenlow, who is enraged and forbids the marriage. On Mr Spenlow's sudden death, the Misses Spenlow, Dora's aunts, become her guardians.

PART 4

Chapters 39–53 (The rise and fall of Heep)

The relationship between Mr Micawber and David becomes uneasy. The Heeps keep a close watch on Agnes and David until Heep learns of David's engagement to Dora.

Mr Peggotty continues to search for Emily but in vain, though he has received letters from her.

Heep hatches a plot to use Maldon to destroy Dr Strong's marriage and involves Mr Wickfield and David. David strikes him in anger. Mr Dick is the means of restoring harmony to the Strongs' marriage.

David becomes a parliamentary reporter as well as being a writer. He is now able to marry Dora, though he soon feels something is missing in their marriage.

Emily has left Steerforth. The stranger, who is haunting Betsey, proves to be her husband. Dora's health deteriorates. Emily is found and Mr Peggotty intends to emigrate to Australia with her.

Mr Micawber confronts Heep with his wickedness in the presence of David, Betsey, Traddles and Mr Dick. Heep has bullied Mr Wickfield into signing illegal documents, trapped Mr Micawber into poverty and forged Mr Wickfield's signature. He is now forced to comply with Traddles's demands. Aunt Betsey's money is recovered and she offers to finance the Micawbers' emigration to Australia.

Dora regrets her inadequacies as a wife just before she dies.

PART 5

Chapters 54–64 (Happy endings)

Betsey's husband is now dead. David returns to Yarmouth to deliver to Ham a letter from Emily. There he witnesses Ham's death in a ferocious storm, while attempting to save Steerforth from a wreck. Steerforth, too, is killed.

The Micawbers, Mr Peggotty, Emily and Mrs Gummidge set sail for Australia.

David travels abroad in despair at his loss of Dora. His thoughts dwell on Agnes, though he feels that he cannot hope to win her love.

He returns home to find Traddles happily married. Mr Dick is working for Traddles and Mr Wickfield is now a contented man.

Creakle has become a magistrate with responsibility for prisons and he invites David and Traddles to meet his model prisoners, Heep and Littimer. David proposes to Agnes, is accepted and they marry. Mr Peggotty returns with news that the emigrants are all doing well. Agnes and David live in perfect happiness together.

Detailed Summaries

Part 1: childhood and education

Chapters 1—4

David's early memories   The opening chapter convincingly conveys the reflections of a mature man on his past life. Because David was born, like Dickens himself, on a Friday, it was expected that he would be unlucky. However, being born with a caul meant that he would be fortunate in life.

The eccentric Betsey has a kind heart.   Aunt Betsey, separated from her violent husband, arrives for David's birth, certain that the baby will be a girl. She treats David's widowed mother, Clara, like a child. She frightens the mild doctor, Mr Chillip, and storms out of the house when she discovers that the baby is a boy.

David's first memories are of his gentle mother, his kindly nurse Peggotty and of his house and garden. Again David's 'meandering' creates an impression of genuine reminiscing. Peggotty is clearly in charge of the household, not Clara Copperfield, but all three are happy together.

Mr Murdstone visits Clara and is immediately disliked by David, but Clara is radiant in his company. Peggotty shares David's dislike of Mr Murdstone and warns Clara about him. The two women are no longer as close as they had been.

Mr Murdstone disliked by everyone but Clara.   Mr Murdstone takes David for a horse-ride and they meet Mr Quinion, whom David will meet again later when he is sent out to work. David notices that Mr Murdstone's friends joke together, but not with him and that Mr Murdstone laughs only once, and that at his own joke about 'Brooks of Sheffield'. We notice Clara's youthful vanity in her questioning of David on his return.

Peggotty is taking David to Yarmouth for a holiday at her brother Dan's when Mr Murdstone arrives and remonstrates with Clara for showing emotion at parting with David.

The kindness of Dan Peggotty's house turns out to be a beached black
Dan Peggotty. barge, and David is charmed by it. Mr Peggotty has taken into his home two orphan children, Ham and Emily, whom he has adopted and a gloomy widow called Mrs Gummidge.

Emily tells of her great affection for Mr Peggotty. She confesses that she would like to be a lady, a desire that will undo her later on. Though he has known her for only a few days, David feels he is in love with her.

David has enjoyed his stay and is devastated at the thought of leaving Emily when the time comes to go. Peggotty is, strangely, trying to subdue David's eagerness to see his mother. On reaching home, David finds that his mother has remarried. Mr Murdstone is controlling her behaviour towards her son. The atmosphere in the house has changed completely.

David is now David now feels unwanted and Clara blames Peggotty
unhappy at home. for her son's rejection of her. Murdstone admonishes Peggotty and threatens David, who is thoroughly convinced that Murdstone will carry out his threats. Clara is afraid to console David.

Miss Murdstone comes to live with them. She takes control of the household and both Murdstones combine to subject Clara and David to their will. By their cruelty, they put David off church and his lessons. His only pleasure now lies in reading, which gives him an escape from the unhappiness of his life and preserves in him a sense of self-worth.

Murdstone is a
sadist masquerad- Mr Murdstone frightens David by showing him a cane;
ing as a moralist. the boy forgets his lessons and Mr Murdstone beats

him unmercifully. David manages to bite Mr Murdstone's hand badly during the beating, which Clara and Peggotty are helpless to prevent. For the next five days, David sees no-one but Miss Murdstone. On the evening of the fifth day, Peggotty informs him that he is to be sent away to a school in London.

COMMENT

The mature David's reminiscences are introduced in a most convincing manner in the opening paragraphs of Chapters 1 and 2. We meet Aunt Betsey, who is to be a major influence in David's life. There is just a hint that, in spite of her brusqueness of manner, she is sympathetic to the needs of others.

The change the Murdstones make to David's once-happy home, transforming it into a hostile and loveless place, is traumatic for David. Mr Murdstone's wink at his sister before thrashing David proves his pose of morality to be a false one.

In all the distress, there are elements of **humour** (see Literary Terms): in Peggotty's buttons flying off (Chapter 2, p. 26) and in the 'Brooks of Sheffield' incident (Chapter 2, p. 31), where the young David is innocently laughing at himself. The bizarre story of David's caul being won in a raffle by an old lady who needed no protection from drowning as she never went near water, is not without its comic aspect (Chapter 1, p. 12).

GLOSSARY

Chapter 1
caul a membrane sometimes covering the head of a new-born infant. It was considered to be a lucky sign
Baboo an Indian gentleman
Begum a Muslim lady of high rank
Dutch clock cheap wooden clock made in Germany

Chapter 2
shaver young fellow

Chapter 3
Yarmouth Bloater a person from Yarmouth

Chapter 4
Disciples a reference to Christ's welcoming of a little child
whom his followers (disciples) were turning away
Roderick Random, Gil Blas, Robinson Crusoe characters
in novels that Dickens himself had enjoyed when
young

CHAPTERS 5–9

David at
Salem House
Barkis interested
in Peggotty.

David leaves home in Barkis's cart on his way to
London via Yarmouth. Barkis questions David about
Peggotty and through him makes an indirect proposal
of marriage to her.

David ill-treated
by adults.

At the coaching inn, David feels very lost and lonely.
The waiter tricks David into giving him most of his
dinner. On the coach, David is the butt of jokes about
his vast appetite. He is squashed between two men on
the journey, with a lady's luggage under his feet. There
is nobody to greet him on his arrival in London.

Mr Mell, a teacher from Salem House, calls eventually
to collect him. Finding that David is hungry, Mr Mell
takes him to buy food to eat at his mother's, who lives

in an almshouse. Mr Mell's appalling flute-playing sends David to sleep after he has breakfasted.

After a sleep on another coach, they arrive at Salem House. It is the school holidays and David is the only boy there.

David is lonely and miserable.

Mell has been ordered to place on David's back a placard with the message, 'Take care of him. He bites'. Tungay, the proprietor's assistant, makes David's life a misery with his bullying. David dreads the return of the other boys.

Creakle is a bully and a sadist.

Creakle, the proprietor, returns to Salem House and David is presented to him. He is harsh and intimidates David. His wife and daughter disapprove of his behaviour. David's request to have the placard removed enrages Creakle.

David meets Traddles who introduces him to the other boys as they return. David also meets Steerforth who impresses him and treats him kindly. Nevertheless, Steerforth takes charge of David's money and dictates how it should be spent, which disconcerts David a little. Steerforth has privileges the others do not have. David learns that Creakle is cruel and ignorant. Steerforth, alone, is immune from his barbaric treatment. Tungay too is cruel. David learns that the teachers are poorly paid and have no status in the school and that the boys believe Miss Creakle is in love with Steerforth.

Dickens's hatred of ill-treatment of children.

Creakle begins the term with a threat of corporal punishment for any slackers. He then strikes David, and other boys as well, with his cane. Traddles suffers more than anyone else from this brutal treatment. His honourable nature is the cause of his being punished for Steerforth's misdemeanour. David's placard is removed, because it protects him from blows of the cane.

David starts to idolise Steerforth, who requests that David tell him the stories he has read, since he,

Steerforth, cannot get to sleep early. At times, David is sleepy, but feels he must carry out Steerforth's wishes. When David receives a parcel from Peggotty, he considers he must give it to Steerforth to share out. In return Steerforth helps David with his schoolwork.

Steerforth's scorn for the poor.

Steerforth is always disparaging Mr Mell. David has told him about the almshouse and is worried Steerforth might use this information against Mell. One day, when the boys are very rowdy, Mr Mell calls for silence, and is insulted by Steerforth. In the midst of the argument, Creakle appears, taking Steerforth's side against Mell.

Traddles alone against Steerforth.

Steerforth discloses that Mell's mother is a pauper. This leads to Mell's dismissal from his post. Creakle praises Steerforth for saving the honour of the school and canes Traddles for sympathising with Mell, but Traddles still accuses Steerforth of treating Mell unjustly. The rest of the boys support Steerforth, after he has promised to send money to Mell, though David still feels guilty.

Steerforth meets the Peggottys

Mr Peggotty and Ham visit David, bringing him food and news of the family. David introduces Steerforth, and the visitors invite him to visit Yarmouth. The first term is now over.

Barkis comes to take David home; he has had no answer from Peggotty to his proposal. Arriving home, David finds his mother nursing a baby. His mother greets him fondly and Peggotty is there too. David is supremely happy, especially as the Murdstones are away for the day.

He notices a difference in his mother; she is not in the best of health and seems anxious. She needs Peggotty's support. David tells them all about Creakle and Steerforth. He nurses the baby and is very happy. This is the last time they are happy together.

PART 1: CHILDHOOD AND EDUCATION

David is used to cow his mother.

By just being there, David is a cause of disturbance in the house. He tries to keep out of the Murdstones' way but is required to join them to enable them to 'train' his mother. Consequently, David is so miserable that he is not sorry to return to Salem House.

One day after breakfast David is called in to see Mrs Creakle, to be given news of his mother's death. Even in his grief, David senses that people are looking on him in a specially sympathetic way, which gives him a certain self-importance. He now leaves Salem House, never to return.

David isolated in his despair.

At Yarmouth Mr Omer, the undertaker, collects David and takes him to his shop to measure him for a mourning suit. David learns now that his baby brother is dead too.

Mr Murdstone is genuinely upset at Clara's death and ignores David, and Miss Murdstone is as cold as ever towards him. The funeral leaves an indelible impression on David. Mr Chillip talks kindly to David, and Peggotty comes to his room to console him. She tells the sad tale of his mother's decline. Peggotty's moving narration brings back to David the image of his mother in his infancy. David thinks of his mother now, flawless and loving, as he first remembered her.

COMMENT

We notice the differences in attitude of Peggotty and Clara when David leaves for London – his mother censorious, Peggotty full of affection. The callousness of sending an eight-year-old boy, on his own, to London to be duped and taken advantage of on the way is beyond belief. The Victorian attitude to children comes across clearly on the coach journey from Yarmouth to London, where his discomfiture is ignored by the adults.

A child's innocent interpretation of the devious actions of others, of the waiter for example, is poignantly described, and David's sense of loneliness and insecurity as he sits waiting to be picked up by Mell is very moving.

Since Creakle is an acquaintance of Murdstone's, it is unsurprising that he should treat David cruelly. The description of Salem House is Dickens's bitter comment on the lack of any control over educational establishments at this time.

David's child-like admiration of his hero, Steerforth, is undiminished by Steerforth's vicious treatment of Mr Mell, while the noble spirit of Traddles is established from the beginning. It is here that Steerforth first meets Emily's family, and the seeds of future tragedy are sown.

Another insight into the attitude of the day towards children is given when David arrives home, not having been told that he has a baby brother, as though it is no business of his.

Mr Murdstone's one saving grace is that he is really upset at the deaths of Clara and the baby, though his total indifference to David's needs cancels this out. Miss Murdstone continues to be totally devoid of any humanity at all.

GLOSSARY   *Chapter 7*
               Alguazil Spanish officer with power to arrest
               wittels victuals, food

CHAPTERS 10–14

David in London and in Dover
David has only Peggotty now.

Miss Murdstone sacks Peggotty. Distressed at leaving Blunderstone, Peggotty takes David with her for a holiday to Yarmouth. She is thinking of marrying Barkis.

At Yarmouth David notices a change in Emily. She

PART 1: CHILDHOOD AND EDUCATION

teases him and knows how to charm Mr Peggotty but she feels for David in his loss. Steerforth is discussed and, as always, highly praised by David. Emily shows a particular interest.

Peggotty's quiet wedding

Barkis continues his silent courtship of Peggotty. One day, Emily and David go on a day's outing with Peggotty and Barkis. Leaving the children outside, Peggotty and Barkis go to church and are married. David protests his undying love for Emily.

At the end of his holiday, Barkis and Peggotty take David home but leave him at the gate and he feels abandoned once more. The Murdstones' attitude to him remains unchanged. David's life is one of empty neglect, but Peggotty comes to see him once a week. These visits and his beloved books are his only consolation.

David's shame and despair.

David is sent to London to work at Murdstone and Grinby's rat-infested and decaying warehouse in Blackfriars, labelling, washing and corking bottles. A sense of deep despair invades David's soul at the bleakness of his future prospects. David is introduced to Mr Micawber, with whom he is to lodge. The Micawbers are constantly pursued by creditors. David is left alone, though only ten years of age, and could easily have turned to crime. He does not fit in with his 'common' workmates and Mr Quinion treats him somewhat differently from the rest.

David shares the Micawbers' troubles.

He feels the worries of the Micawbers, with whom he is very friendly, and offers them money from the pittance he has. Mr Micawber is imprisoned for debt; all his furniture is sold and his family move into prison with him, but David stays in contact with them.

David's honesty is evident here.

The Micawbers are freed from prison and leave for Plymouth, leaving David friendless. David decides to run away to his Aunt Betsey's. He learns from Peggotty that his aunt lives near Dover and borrows half a guinea from her. In trying to organise delivery of his belongings to Dover, David has both his box and half-guinea stolen.

David runs away

Almost penniless, David is still determined to continue on to Dover. On the road, he is a lamb among wolves, lonely and frightened of the people he meets. Nearing Dover, David is directed to Betsey's.

Betsey's kind heart

Is Mr Dick sane?

David arrives at Betsey's in a terrible state. At first she tells him to go away but, finding who he is, brings him in and looks after him. We meet Mr Dick, a simple-minded man whom Betsey has saved from an asylum, and whose advice she defiantly values.

Betsey stands by David against the Murdstones.

Betsey is always chasing donkeys away from her door and the Murdstones arrive on donkeys, thus bringing about an immediate confrontation. Mr Murdstone lays down an ultimatum that David goes back with him at once, or is in future the responsibility of Betsey. David begs to be allowed to stay. Mr Dick is in favour of David's staying and Aunt Betsey decides to keep him. She does not believe a word the Murdstones say about David and tells them plainly what she thinks of them. Betsey and Mr Dick are to be joint guardians of David. His new life is marked with a new name: Trotwood Copperfield.

COMMENT

After Peggotty has been sacked, David knows the Murdstones would like to get rid of him, too, if they could. He is utterly alone, and his future is bleak.

During the brief interval at Yarmouth, we notice that Emily is growing up and using her feminine wiles on Mr Peggotty, and that everybody spoils her. It is evident that she is fascinated by the story of Steerforth – a pointer to the future.

David's experience at Murdstone and Grinby's reflects Dickens's own despair and misery at the blacking

PART 1: CHILDHOOD AND EDUCATION

factory and the account of David's feelings therefore rings true. David comes across as considerate and responsible beyond his years, when he tries to help the Micawbers. Another reference to Dickens's own family's experience is contained in the Micawbers' imprisonment for debt. This, surely, is an indictment of the conditions of the poor, who have no means of controlling their own lives.

The way the innocent child, David, is preyed upon by people, who are themselves poor, Dolloby, Charley and the tinker, presents us with a chilling view of life among the poor in Victorian England. Even those he asks the way use him as the butt of their jokes and have no feeling for his distress, as though the child had no status in society.

Betsey is seen to hide a kind heart beneath her abrupt manner by defending David against the Murdstones and taking him in. Her deference to the opinions of the simple-minded Mr Dick is a demonstration of her sensitivity also.

GLOSSARY

Chapter 12
half a guinea 10s 6d (a guinea was worth one pound and one shilling)
tanner an old sixpence
pollis police

Chapter 13
slop-shops shops that sold cheap ready made clothing
Half a crown coin worth one eighth of £1
shilling one twentieth of £1
lay method of stealing
prig thief

Chapter 14
a natural a half-wit from birth

CHAPTERS 15–18

*David at
school in
Canterbury*

David gets on extremely well with Aunt Betsey and Mr
Dick, who spends his life writing his Memorial and
flying its messages on a great kite.

*David's good
angel and his
enemy.*

Betsey takes David to Mr Wickfield's to get advice on a
good school for David. He has his first meeting with
Uriah Heep, whose appearance is as repulsive as his
later actions prove his character to be. Mr Wickfield's
handsome looks are in accord with his nobility of
character. While Mr Wickfield and Betsey are visiting
the proposed school, David is uncomfortable in the
presence of Uriah Heep.

Betsey is happy with Dr Strong's school, and Mr
Wickfield offers to lodge David at his own house. Now
David meets Agnes, Mr Wickfield's daughter, whose
calm manner makes an immediate impression on him,
which is to last him his life through. David is delighted
with his accommodation but Aunt Betsey is upset at
leaving him.

Dr Strong, principal of the school, has a pretty young
wife, Annie. He wants Mr Wickfield to find a post for
her cousin, Jack Maldon, and Wickfield suspects that
Dr Strong wishes to be rid of Maldon.

The appearance of the school is as pleasant as the
welcome David receives. Because of the hardships he
has suffered, David feels older than the other boys,
though academically they are mostly ahead of him. He
fears they might learn about the sordidness of his past.

*Maldon a danger
to the Strongs'
marriage.*

Mr Wickfield praises Dr Strong's character, but dislikes
Maldon and is keen to get him away somewhere. David
soon comes to admire Agnes for her radiant goodness.
Mr Wickfield cannot bear to be separated from his
daughter, though he wonders whether she becomes
bored living with him.

PART 1: CHILDHOOD AND EDUCATION

Heep sees David as a usurper.

Heep is studying law. It is in his mind that David will become Mr Wickfield's partner.

David settles in at Dr Strong's school and works hard there. It is a happy place, appealing to all that is noble in the boys. Dr Strong is a kind and innocent man, loved by the boys but easily abused by rogues, from whom boys and masters try to protect him. He has been married to twenty-year-old Annie for only a year.

Mrs Markleham seeks to gain favours for her family.

Annie is always kind to David, but keeps her distance from Mr Wickfield. Jack Maldon is to go to India and a farewell party is held at Dr Strong's. Annie's mother, Mrs Markleham, embarrasses her daughter by looking for favours for her family. Annie is worried about something and is not her old self. Mrs Markleham hints that Dr Strong should continue to support Maldon.

By chance, David observes Dr Strong and Annie together and is moved by seeing the closeness of their relationship.

David has kept in touch with Peggotty and now can repay the money he has borrowed from her. Peggotty tells him that his old house is to be let or sold and the Murdstones have gone. Aunt Betsey keeps an eye on David through frequent visits at unusual times. Mr Dick also makes regular visits to David and reports that a man hides near the house and frightens Betsey, who is seen to give him money.

Mr Dick and Dr Strong become friends.

Mr Dick is popular with the boys at the school. He is also accepted by Annie and Dr Strong, for whom he has the greatest respect.

David is invited to the Heeps' ''umble' home. Both Heeps question David closely, worming information out of him that he is loath to give.

Mr Micawber arrives

David is saved by the unexpected arrival of Mr Micawber. He was not well received at Plymouth by his wife's family and is now at a Canterbury hotel, waiting for money from London to pay the bill.

Heep's friendship with Micawber will have important consequences.

Mr Micawber has made a friend of Heep. David is worried about what Mr Micawber might tell Heep about him. On their last evening in Canterbury, the Micawbers are thoroughly happy, but on their return to London, Mr Micawber writes to David about his hopeless financial situation.

David falls in love twice – first with Miss Shepherd, and later with Miss Larkins.

He fights a young butcher of Canterbury, who makes a nuisance of himself to the boys at Dr Strong's. David is soundly beaten by the butcher and consoled by Agnes. He becomes head boy at school. After being taunted again by the butcher, David defeats him and resumes his normal life-style.

COMMENT

David has a happy home at Aunt Betsey's for the first time since the Murdstones came into his life.

At Mr Wickfield's, he meets the girl who will influence him for good for the rest of his life. On the other hand, it is here too that he meets Heep, who plots against Mr Wickfield and Dr Strong and implicates David. In Chapter 15 reference is first made to Mr Wickfield's drinking, which makes him vulnerable to Heep's wiles.

In Dr Strong, we see another example of goodness and innocence taken advantage of by the unscrupulous and the scheming.

Mrs Markleham is always trying to gain favours for her family and has the gift, to the ultimate degree, of embarrassing her daughter before others. On the night Maldon is to set off for India, Annie Strong is distressed and is unable to sing. Mr Wickfield

PART 1: CHILDHOOD AND EDUCATION

suspects something is going on between Maldon and Annie.

Betsey takes her responsibility for David's schooling seriously, but finding all is well at Dr Strong's school, she ceases to visit. Mr Dick's continued visits to the school forge a bond between him and the Strongs that will play an important part later in the novel.

The budding friendship between Mr Micawber and Heep, on Mr Micawber's return from Plymouth, will lead to a dramatic confrontation between them both later on, which will result in the rescue of Mr Wickfield from Heep's clutches.

The humorous passages about Miss Shepherd and Miss Larkins show a prominent facet of David's character – his habit of falling in – and out of – love.

GLOSSARY

Chapter 18

spencer lady's short jacket drawing attention to the shape of the bust

the stocks a device for holding an offender by the feet; a position of disgrace

Identify the speaker.

4 'There are people enought to tread upon me in my lowly state, without my doing outrage to their feelings by possessing learning. Learning ain't for me. A person like myself had better not aspire'

1 'David Copperfield all over! David Copperfield from head to foot! Calls a house a rookery when there's not a rook near it'

2 'David, if I have an obstinate horse or dog to deal with, what do you think I do? I beat him. I make him wince, and smart'

3 'I am a determined character. That's what I am. I do my duty. That's what *I* do. My flesh and blood when it rises against me is not my flesh and blood. I discard it'

Think about the circumstances in which these words are said and what they tell us of the characters of the speakers.

Check your answers on page 96.

 Consider these issues.

a The methods Dickens uses to convince us that David is really looking back on a past life and that it is not just a fiction.

b The character of Betsey and any change in her portrayal you have noticed up to Chapter 18.

c Whether the behaviour of the Murdstones is motivated by sadistic tendencies or by moral values, and how you can tell.

d The number of associations, which will become important later on, and insights into characters, which become clear only as the novel progresses.

e How Dickens introduces humour into the novel, sometimes in an expression, sometimes in a character or situation.

f What we learn of David's character in Part 1.

g Whether there are any moral messages which Dickens is attempting to convey to the audience of his day.

PART 2: STEERFORTH AGAIN; DORA

CHAPTERS 19—22

David in London

David leaves school without knowing what he would like to do, and Mr Dick has no sensible advice to offer him.

Betsey trying to make David independent.

Betsey urges David to be 'a firm fellow' (Chapter 19, p. 259) and plans to send him on his own to Suffolk and London, thinking it might help him to make up his mind about a career.

David visits Agnes first, who tells him of her father's deteriorating health. There is a great tenderness of feeling between her and her father. All three call on Dr Strong, who intends to retire.

Suspicions about Maldon and Annie.

At Dr Strong's house, Mrs Markleham, the 'Old Soldier', convinces Dr Strong that he should find Maldon a post at home on grounds of ill-health. Mr Wickfield does not accept Maldon's reasons for returning. David shares Mr Wickfield's suspicions about Annie and is very depressed at the thought of treachery against Dr Strong.

David has not yet developed 'firmness' of character.

On the stagecoach from Canterbury, David shows his lack of firmness by the ease with which he is persuaded to give up his seat. The coach retraces David's journey on foot from London.

At the London inn, David tries to appear manly before the waiter, but is patronised by him. He meets Steerforth, who is now at Oxford. Steerforth's manner with the waiter is in stark contrast to David's diffident attitude. He orders the waiter peremptorily to move David to a better room next to his.

David is conscious of his inexperience, while Steerforth expects preferential treatment. He invites David to his home at Highgate.

Steerforth at home

At Highgate, David meets Mrs Steerforth and Rosa Dartle, her companion, who has a habit of casting doubt on what people say by her pretended ignorance. David learns that Steerforth scarred her face with a hammer when he was a boy. David invites Steerforth down to Suffolk to see the Peggottys. Steerforth is very disparaging about them; David believes he is joking, but he is in earnest. Mrs Steerforth is obsessed with her son and welcomes David because he too idolises her son. Steerforth's personal servant, Littimer, makes David feel like a little boy.

David blind to Steerforth's real character.

David and Steerforth leave for Yarmouth and any derogatory remarks Steerforth makes about the place David interprets as compliments.

At Yarmouth David learns that Emily is apprenticed to Mr Omer's workshop. The local women gossip about her pretensions to be a lady and are jealous of her. David's reunion with Peggotty is an emotional one. He receives a hearty welcome from Barkis, too, who is full of praise for Peggotty's baking. He pretends to be a poor man and claims that his box of money is full of old clothes.

Steerforth charms Emily.

On his visit Steerforth charms Peggotty as he has charmed David. He sleeps at the hotel, while David stays at Peggotty's. They both arrive at Mr Peggotty's a moment after the announcement of Ham's engagement to Emily. David finds Ham's evident true love for Emily and his understanding of his own deficiencies extremely moving. Steerforth, as usual, takes over the proceedings, charming everybody. Having left the house, however, Steerforth shows his true colours by sneering at Ham. David, still blind to reality, sees it as a joke.

Steerforth's guilty feelings.

During the course of their holiday, the two friends are often separated by their diverging interests and

Steerforth does not tell David what he has been doing. One night on his return from a visit to Blunderstone, David discovers Steerforth alone at Mr Peggotty's, musing before the fire. He starts guiltily at David's interruption and seems angry. He is pale 'even to his lips' (Chapter 22, p. 304) as he announces that Littimer is at Yarmouth.

When Steerforth and David meet Ham and Emily, Emily withdraws her hand from Ham's arm, blushing, an ominous portent if only Ham knew it. A young woman, Martha Endell, is observed to follow Emily. Steerforth sees her black figure as an **image** (see Literary Terms) of his own black deed about to be committed.

Miss Mowcher hints at Steerforth's plans.

Miss Mowcher, a hairdresser and beautician, arrives to see Steerforth. She treats Steerforth like a child, but amidst the banter, she makes a number of telling statements implying that she knows what Steerforth is up to.

Emily feels she is not good enough for Ham.

Martha is talking to Emily in private. Emily gives money from Ham to Martha to help her go to London. Emily protests that she is not as good to Ham as he is to her and is greatly distressed. She leaves with him, apparently close and loving.

COMMENT   David has a fairy-tale vision of the world outside school
                     and feels he will achieve great things, though he has no
                     idea in what field. Betsey is embarrassed in showing her
                     affection for him and her pride in him.

                     Mrs Markleham rides rough-shod over her daughter's
                     feelings in her efforts to manipulate Dr Strong to the
                     benefit of her family. David is finding that people are
                     not deceived by his efforts to be worldly-wise and take
                     advantage of his youthfulness. He makes the tragic
                     decision to invite Steerforth to Yarmouth. He is totally
                     blind to Steerforth's contempt for ordinary people.

                     It is significant that even Mr Omer admits that Emily
                     can be wayward and perhaps there is some truth in
                     what the local women think of her. Steerforth's
                     hypocrisy, unseen by David, is evident from his
                     friendliness to Ham in his company and his sneering
                     comments about him afterwards.

                     For all her bonhomie, Miss Mowcher is astute.
                     Steerforth shows no reaction to her probing statements.

                     On the surface, there does not seem evidence enough to
                     cause so much distress to Emily that she is on the point
                     of breakdown. In these chapters Dickens stresses the
                     difference between how things appear on the surface,
                     and the reality beneath.

GLOSSARY   *Chapter 22*
                     cupper person skilled in drawing blood from the body by the
                     use of a vacuum glass (cupping-glass) applied to a cut in the
                     skin

CHAPTERS 23–25

David to be a   Littimer is left behind when Steerforth and David leave
proctor   for home. Aunt Betsey, in a letter, has suggested that
                     David might like to be a proctor. Steerforth explains to

PART 2: STEERFORTH AGAIN; DORA

David what a proctor does, and he feels inclined to take up such a profession. Betsey is pleased about David's decision and happy to provide the thousand pounds it will cost. David feels very guilty about this large expense, but Betsey is determined.

Spenlow and Jorkins

On their way to Spenlow and Jorkins in Doctors' Commons, a 'sturdy beggar' appears and Betsey, to David's astonishment, goes with him and gives him ten guineas. Mr Spenlow greets them and arranges fee and conditions, blaming his partner, Jorkins, for their rigidity; there is no salary forthcoming. Jorkins's name is always used by Mr Spenlow in awkward situations. Aunt Betsey arranges lodgings for David at Mrs Crupp's.

Agnes warns David against Steerforth.

David enjoys his independence, but is lonely. He is still obsessed with Steerforth, who has not been to see him. When he finally arrives, David invites him and his friends to dinner, where they consume a great amount of wine and David becomes very drunk. They all go to the theatre where David sees Agnes in the audience. Seeing the condition David is in, she persuades him and his companions to go home. The next morning, David is full of shame for the previous night's conduct.

Agnes asks David to come and see her. She does not upbraid him for his drunkenness, but she does warn him against Steerforth.

Heep in partnership with Mr Wickfield.

The devastating news that Agnes brings is that Heep is going to be her father's partner. Mr Wickfield is afraid of Heep, who has some kind of hold upon him. Agnes is very distressed, since she feels she has betrayed her father by advising him to accept Heep as his partner. She wants David to be friendly towards Heep.

David is invited to dinner at the Waterbrooks' where Agnes is staying and finds Heep among the guests. He

haunts David for the rest of the evening, observing
closely any conversation he has with Agnes.

Heep declares his
love for Agnes.

Among the 'icy' guests, there is one whom David
welcomes – Traddles, who is reading for the bar.
Traddles and David exchange addresses and promise
to meet again. David is still singing the praises of
Steerforth, though he cannot persuade Agnes to join
him. Heep hovers closely all evening. David's irritation
with him changes to fury as Heep admits the feelings
he has towards Agnes. He threatens David with
moral blackmail to ensure his secret is kept. David
has the misfortune of having to put Heep up for the
night.

COMMENT

We have no real evidence as yet to make the connection
between Littimer's staying at Yarmouth and
Steerforth's unusual silence on his journey home.
Dickens's opinion of the judicial system in Chapter 23
is that it is cosy, self-aggrandising, greedy, hypocritical
and very out of date.

The first crack, though a slight one, in David's defence
of Steerforth is due to Agnes, his 'good angel'. Upon
seeing David's rooms, Steerforth's first thought is that
they can be useful to him as a town base.

The meeting with Traddles is one of many coincidences
which run throughout the novel. Dickens holds up to
ridicule the social graces of the time, when David
thinks they would all enjoy themselves better if they
weren't so genteel.

The first time Agnes cries is here, as she relates the
news of Heep taking over from her father. In this
section, the shadow of Heep falls across the novel in a
sinister way, whereas previously he has been repulsive
but harmless. He has achieved his first ambition. Now
he is after his second – the hand of Agnes.

PART 2: STEERFORTH AGAIN; DORA

GLOSSARY   *Chapter 24*
             Lares Roman household deities

CHAPTERS 26–30

Old friends and a new love

Heep sees David as a rival for the hand of Agnes and David fears Agnes might in time sacrifice herself to Heep for her father's sake. Now articled to Spenlow and Jorkins, he is invited to Mr Spenlow's house to celebrate. Dickens comments on the greed and self-serving practices of the legal profession here.

David loses his judgement when in love.

At Spenlow's, David is introduced to Dora and is at once overwhelmed and thinks he loves Dora 'to distraction!' (Chapter 26, p. 362). His distraction is so great that he is not surprised to find that Miss Murdstone is Dora's 'confidential friend' and companion. She calls for a truce between David and herself, which he accepts, though he tells her what he thinks of her.

Once again Dickens makes use of coincidence.

David sets out to find Traddles, who is living in great poverty. He is engaged to a curate's daughter in Devonshire but has no prospect of marrying her. To David's amazement, Traddles's landlord turns out to be Mr Micawber.

Littimer's strange ignorance of Steerforth's whereabouts.

David invites Traddles and the Micawbers to dinner. The dinner is a disaster at first, but is redeemed by Mr Micawber, until Littimer's arrival casts a gloom over the company. He is hesitant when questioned by David about Steerforth and Yarmouth, and departs in a hurry.

The Micawbers are in straitened circumstances, and Mrs Micawber blames society for not appreciating her husband's talents.

Steerforth again mocks a good person – Traddles.

David warns Traddles not to lend Micawber any money. Steerforth makes his appearance, and David's doubts about him dissolve. On David's mentioning Traddles, Steerforth's reply is uncomplimentary. He has come from Yarmouth and brings a letter to David from Peggotty, with the news that Barkis is dying. When David proposes to go to Yarmouth the next day to see Peggotty, Steerforth persuades him to spend a day at his mother's house first.

Rosa suspicious about Steerforth's doings.

Mrs Steerforth and Rosa Dartle are pleased to see David, but Rosa is scrutinising him in a peculiar fashion, which he finds discomfiting. She is suspicious about Steerforth's recent absence from home. Steerforth makes a special effort to charm her. Rosa relaxes enough to play the harp and sing, until Steerforth puts his arm around her, whereat she throws him off violently and runs out of the room.

Steerforth admires the goodness in David.

Steerforth values David's friendship but hints at a future separation. As David leaves, he is, unknowingly, leaving his friend forever.

In Yarmouth, Mr Omer tells David that Emily is unsettled; he has noticed the change in her and so have others. Barkis's illness has delayed her marriage to Ham.

Emily distances herself from Ham.

Barkis is now close to death. Emily is clinging closer and closer to her uncle and, when meeting David, her conduct is strange and nervous. Rather than let Ham take her home, she prefers to stay with Mr Peggotty and Ham acquiesces. David thinks Emily's dread of death is the cause of her odd behaviour.

Barkis continues a miser to the end, but he smiles at David as he breathes his last.

COMMENT   In Heep's mind, David is an obstacle to all his evil aims, which lie hidden under his mask of humility.

Where Dora is concerned, David abandons all reasoning and is a complete slave to her beauty; this blinds him to the possibility that they might not be suited.

Coincidences abound in this novel. Notice what use Dickens makes of this device.

It is **symbolic** (see Literary Terms) that Littimer changes the atmosphere at the dinner party from gaiety to gloom, since he has just been arranging the elopement of Emily and Steerforth.

Traddles is a character of pure goodness, yet Steerforth sneers at him behind his back just as he does at Ham, who is equally good. This sheds some light on the character of Steerforth. Does he admire David, because David admires him?

GLOSSARY   *Chapter 26*
phaeton an open carriage
cardamums aromatic spice

Chapter 28
a bill probably a bond on which cash could be raised

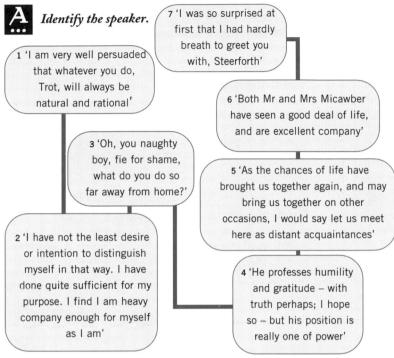

A *Identify the speaker.*

7 'I was so surprised at first that I had hardly breath to greet you with, Steerforth'

1 'I am very well persuaded that whatever you do, Trot, will always be natural and rational'

6 'Both Mr and Mrs Micawber have seen a good deal of life, and are excellent company'

3 'Oh, you naughty boy, fie for shame, what do you do so far away from home?'

5 'As the chances of life have brought us together again, and may bring us together on other occasions, I would say let us meet here as distant acquaintances'

2 'I have not the least desire or intention to distinguish myself in that way. I have done quite sufficient for my purpose. I find I am heavy company enough for myself as I am'

4 'He professes humility and gratitude – with truth perhaps; I hope so – but his position is really one of power'

Can you remember the circumstances under which the quotations were spoken?

Check your answers on page 96.

B *Consider these issues.*

a The circumstances that cast suspicion on Annie Strong.

b The differences in attitude to life between David and Steerforth.

c Information given about Emily in this part.

d Hints in the text which point to future events.

e The role of Miss Mowcher.

f Comments upon the judicial system in the novel.

PART 3: EMILY LOST; DAVID AND DORA

CHAPTERS 31–32

Emily elopes with Steerforth

The news of the elopement is shattering.

After the funeral, Peggotty, David, Emily and Ham have arranged to meet at the old boathouse. Ham comes by himself in great distress, however: Emily has eloped with Steerforth.

Even Mrs Gummidge forgets her self-pity in consoling Mr Peggotty, and David feels a responsibility for having introduced Steerforth to the family.

David cannot bring himself to despise Steerforth.

In his own heart, David still feels admiration for Steerforth's good qualities, though he now sees his true character. In his mind he distinguishes between his sorrow at the betrayal and his lack of anger against the traitor. David fears for Steerforth's life if Ham ever finds him.

Mrs Gummidge is a changed woman now and will keep the house ready for Emily's return while Dan Peggotty is searching for her.

Miss Mowcher misled.

Mr Omer takes the news so badly that he falls ill and his daughter thinks there was never any good in Emily, yet she weeps for her, too. Miss Mowcher arrives, greatly upset, though, earlier, she seemed to hint at this very event. She had been misled by Steerforth and thought that David was in love with Emily, and was used by Steerforth to communicate with the girl. She has learnt that Emily and Steerforth have gone abroad, but she will watch for their return and inform David.

Mrs Steerforth disowns her son.

Mr Peggotty begins his journey at Mrs Steerforth's, who already knows what has happened and is very upset herself at her son's social disgrace. There is no common ground between her and Mr Peggotty. Rosa is incensed and shows her jealousy and contempt for both Emily and Mr Peggotty. Mr Peggotty's affection for Emily is unchanged.

COMMENT   Though there have been various hints that Emily is not wholly perfect, her elopement with Steerforth has a staggering effect upon the reader, and is one of the points of high drama in the novel. Yet it does not alienate David from his hero entirely. The noble characters of Ham and Mr Peggotty are seen in contrast to the self-seeking Steerforth.

CHAPTERS 33–35

David's infatuation

David is still love-sick for Dora, whom he sees unrealistically as an angel, and he spends hours walking around outside her house. He confides his love to Peggotty.

In the course of helping her with legal matters, he shows Peggotty the sights of London. At Doctors' Commons, they meet Mr Murdstone, who is about to marry a young heiress.

Dickens's contempt for the legal system.

In the justice system, those who do the least work are richly rewarded; those who do most are least paid and regarded. Spenlow approves of this exploitation.

David is ecstatic when invited to Dora's birthday picnic. He meets her friend, Miss Mills, who has adopted an air of world-weariness at the age of twenty.

Mr Spenlow ignorant of Dora's behaviour.

Julia Mills acts as the match-maker to bring Dora and David together and invites David to meet Dora at her house. When the two lovers are alone, David declares his love which Dora accepts: they are engaged. When they have their first quarrel, Julia acts as go-between to heal the rift. David writes to Agnes about his engagement and receives a warm letter in reply.

Traddles's innate goodness.

Peggotty is staying with David, a fact which angers Mrs Crupp, who now refuses to do any work for him.

PART 3: EMILY LOST; DAVID AND DORA

Traddles visits and has heard about Dora; David hears
of Traddles's fiancée, Sophy, who looks after all her
family. Traddles's treasured possessions have gone to
pay Mr Micawber's bills. David arranges, through
Peggotty, to buy them back, on condition that Traddles
lend no more money to Mr Micawber.

*Aunt Betsey
ruined*

Aunt Betsey and Mr Dick arrive unexpectedly at
David's rooms, together with an amount of luggage. It
transpires that Betsey is ruined, though she does not
worry about herself, but only about David.

Mr Dick has no idea why Betsey is ruined and is in
tears when David explains to him the consequences
of poverty. Aunt Betsey settles in and appreciates
Peggotty's company and her offer of money, which
she declines to accept. She gently enquires about
Dora's character, obviously hoping she is not a replica
of David's mother. David professes his love for his
fiancée, while Betsey remains reserved, wondering
silently why he doesn't feel for Agnes the way he feels
for Dora.

*David's selfish
attitude.*

His poverty seems to David to threaten his proposed
marriage; at first he thinks not of his aunt, but of
himself. On reflection, however, he tries to cancel his
articles, but Mr Spenlow, and Mr Jorkins, refuses to
refund the money paid as premium.

Agnes arrives in London to see Aunt Betsey. She is
accompanied by her father and Heep. The Heeps are
now living at Mr Wickfield's and intrude on the
closeness of father and daughter.

*The dark shadow
of Heep.*

Betsey is determined that David will be a proctor and,
by a strange coincidence, Agnes tells David that Dr
Strong now lives in London and requires a part-time
secretary – a ready-made job for David, to help his
finances.

When Mr Wickfield and Heep arrive, David is struck by the role-reversal he finds, and by the sad change in Mr Wickfield. Heep appears to be happy at David's downfall. Betsey loses patience with him and puts him in his place. Mr Wickfield pretends that Heep is an asset to him, but when Heep leaves, Mr Wickfield seems happier, more like his old self.

COMMENT   David is besotted with Dora to a degree difficult for the reader to understand on the evidence available. He has lost his judgement altogether. The **melodramatic** (see Literary Terms) Miss Mills plays the role of intermediary between the lovers both here and in the following chapters. This is her purpose in the novel. The goodness of Traddles comes across well at this stage; he has no trace of selfishness in him and so is easily used by Mr Micawber.

Betsey's concern for David is evident here; she takes her responsibility for him very seriously. She can see what David cannot: that he should marry Agnes, not anyone else. Uriah Heep looms over the Wickfields like a menacing shadow. He is delighted at David's financial problems because he thinks this gives him an advantage over David.

CHAPTERS $36-38$

David's devotion to Dora

David is employed by Dr Strong, who is still exploited by Jack Maldon. Maldon shows a supercilious and callous attitude towards the tragedies of others. In this, David considers him typical of his class. The innocent Dr Strong encourages his wife to go out with Maldon but she is successful in cancelling a proposed visit to the opera.

David wants to be a journalist and decides to learn shorthand for that purpose. Traddles is surprised at the strength of David's determination. Traddles kindly finds paid work for Mr Dick, so that he feels he is supporting Betsey.

Mr Micawber employed by Heep

Uriah Heep has engaged Mr Micawber as his confidential clerk and the family are to move up to Canterbury. Mr Micawber becomes puffed up with ambitious pride about what he might now become. When David gives the Micawbers news of his aunt's financial problems, they are quite elated; the news seems to make them 'comfortable and friendly' (Chapter 36, p. 493). Traddles's loan to Mr Micawber is 'paid off' with an i.o.u.

Dora's inability to face the real world.

David lets Dora know that he is ruined, but is so eloquent in protesting his love for her that he calms her initial fears and their relationship continues. His suggestions that she should learn a little about house-keeping put her in a faint, but Miss Mills brings her round.

David determined not to give up Dora.

David is still intent on becoming a parliamentary reporter, but finds shorthand difficult to master: Traddles helps by dictating speeches to him.

Miss Murdstone has discovered David's love letters to Dora and shows them to her father. Mr Spenlow is enraged but David refuses to consent to give Dora up, and therefore Mr Spenlow is to attempt to change Dora's mind. In Mr Spenlow's eyes, money is more important than love, where marriage is concerned.

The next morning David is informed of Mr Spenlow's sudden death. Though Mr Spenlow had told David his financial affairs were long since arranged, nobody can find a will, since he hasn't left one, and his assets amount to no more than a thousand pounds.

Through Miss Mills, David finds that Dora's maiden aunts are to look after her at their home in Putney. He draws consolation from Miss Mills, who keeps a diary on Dora's state of mind.

COMMENT   Maldon is an incompetent, lazy, self-seeking man, and Dr Strong's encouragement of his wife to go out with him against her own wishes, beggars belief.

Heep, unknowingly, by employing Mr Micawber in a confidential capacity, is sowing the seeds of his own destruction.

Since David is so practical at times, it is difficult to understand how he can seriously lose his head over Dora, who is so spoiled and impractical as to be totally unreal. There is some truth in Mr Spenlow's words that it is all 'youthful nonsense' (Chapter 38, p. 511).

The device of Mr Spenlow's sudden and opportune death is, to say the least, unconvincing, but it does help along the plot (see Literary Terms).

GLOSSARY   *Chapter 38*
pinions wings

Identify the speaker.

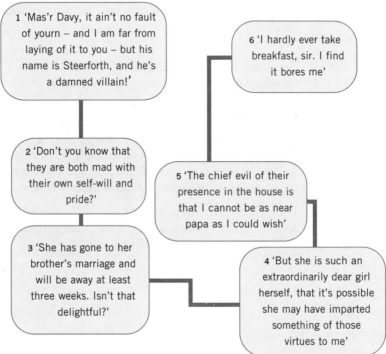

1 'Mas'r Davy, it ain't no fault of yourn – and I am far from laying of it to you – but his name is Steerforth, and he's a damned villain!'

6 'I hardly ever take breakfast, sir. I find it bores me'

2 'Don't you know that they are both mad with their own self-will and pride?'

5 'The chief evil of their presence in the house is that I cannot be as near papa as I could wish'

3 'She has gone to her brother's marriage and will be away at least three weeks. Isn't that delightful?'

4 'But she is such an extraordinarily dear girl herself, that it's possible she may have imparted something of those virtues to me'

Think about the circumstances in which these words are said and what they tell us of the character of the speakers or their subjects.

Check your answers on page 96.

 Consider these issues.

a David's altered attitude to Steerforth.

b Mrs Steerforth's views on the elopement.

c Mr Spenlow's opinion of the justice system contrasted with David's views.

d The association of Traddles and Micawber.

e The coincidences that occur in the novel.

f Dora's reaction to David's financial difficulties.

PART 4: THE RISE AND FALL OF HEEP

CHAPTERS 39–42

Heep's revenge on Mrs Strong

Criticism of the practices of the courts.

Jorkins's business is doing badly since Mr Spenlow's death. David comments upon the sharp practices of the lawyers, which have a farcical effect upon himself at one point.

David visits the Wickfields. Mr Micawber is now in Heep's old office and is living in Heep's former home. David questions Mr Micawber who cannot really be open with him and is not at ease. He is, however, full of praise for Agnes and, like Betsey, wonders why David does not court her.

David's dependence on Agnes.

David needs Agnes's support and advice and tells her so. She advises him to be open with Dora's guardians about his love for her and to let the ladies know that he will abide by their conditions.

Mr Wickfield's room is a symbol of himself, having been stripped of a number of items which have been transferred to Heep's new room. Even in his domestic matters, Mr Wickfield is completely subservient to Heep now.

The Heeps keep watch.

Both Heeps are constantly spying on the household, which creates a depressing atmosphere. Heep admits he and his mother are spying on David because he is seen as a dangerous rival for the hand of Agnes. He promises to discontinue this activity on hearing that David has a fiancée. Uriah taunts Mr Wickfield with his designs on Agnes and enrages him. Mr Wickfield accuses Heep of destroying him and is subdued by Heep's threats.

David warns Agnes not to sacrifice herself for the sake of her father. Uriah tells David he has made it up with Mr Wickfield, but admits he is still after Agnes.

PART 4: THE RISE AND FALL OF HEEP

Aunt Betsey is extremely worried by these events. David writes to the Misses Spenlow asking to be permitted to visit Dora.

Mr Peggotty still searching for Emily.

By chance, one snowy night David sees Martha Endell in the street and immediately afterwards meets Mr Peggotty, aged and unkempt, still looking for Emily. While Mr Peggotty is telling his tale to David, Martha is secretly listening. Mr Peggotty is fully convinced that he will bring Emily home. She has written to Mrs Gummidge and sent money, which Mr Peggotty refuses to accept.

Ham doesn't care whether he lives or dies, but busies himself in work and helping others.

Dora's guardians ask David to visit them and he decides to take Traddles with him. The Misses Spenlow are very formal, but they receive them courteously. David is allowed to visit three times a week, but the Spenlow sisters want to meet Betsey.

David reunited with Dora

David is allowed to see Dora now but she is unhappy about Traddles's presence and the proposed visit by Betsey.

Aunt Betsey does not share David's delight with the arrangements; something is preying on her mind, though she is glad he is happy.

Betsey's visits to the Spenlows are on foot and at unusual times, which does not conform to the sisters' idea of decorum. Dora is treated by everyone as a pet and she bursts into tears when David refers to this. Her response mirrors that of Clara to Peggotty earlier on. Efforts to help her to be practical end in failure and David too begins to treat her like a toy.

Heep's revenge on Annie and Maldon

Agnes and her father visit Dr Strong for a fortnight and have to bring Mrs Heep along with them to London. Uriah follows next day. It appears he has nursed for a long time a grudge against Annie and Maldon and now he threatens the Strongs' marriage, by hinting at an affair between Maldon and Annie.

David takes Agnes to meet Dora, and the visit is a great success. During the visit, Agnes assures David that she is not going to be blackmailed by Heep.

Heep accuses Annie.

When David is about to leave Dr Strong's, he notices Heep and Mr Wickfield in Dr Strong's room, Mr Wickfield in some distress. Heep has told Dr Strong that his wife has been having an affair with Maldon for a long time. He puts pressure on Mr Wickfield to corroborate his story. Heep now uses David as a witness and he is embroiled against his will.

In his generosity of spirit, Dr Strong feels that he has failed Annie, not she him.

David strikes Heep.

When they are alone together, David takes Heep to task for trapping him in the argument against Annie and, in a fury, strikes Heep across the face. Heep pretends he is not an enemy and David cannot shake him off, since Heep follows him.

A change has come over Annie, though Dr Strong has not confronted her with his knowledge, and the doctor is visibly ageing.

Mr Dick restores the happiness of the Strongs.

With Mr Dick's help Mrs Strong shows her husband her love for him, and trust is restored between husband and wife. Meanwhile, Mrs Micawber writes to David that she is very concerned about changes that have taken place in her husband's character; obviously she is in need of help.

COMMENT

Dickens uses a humorous situation to make fun of the sharp practices of lawyers in his day. Heep is as evil as he is repulsive and has three objectives in mind: taking over Mr Wickfield's firm, which he has achieved; avenging supposed slights on him by Annie and

PART 4: THE RISE AND FALL OF HEEP

Maldon, by persuading Dr Strong that they are having an affair; and forcing Agnes to marry him by blackmailing her. He will use anybody and any means to achieve his ends.

In contrast we observe the perseverance of Mr Peggotty, tirelessly searching for Emily, and we admire his selfless love, forgiveness and concern for her welfare.

It seems that, though David is blind as to whom he should marry, this is blatantly obvious to others. The love of Dr Strong for his wife is exemplary and we begin to see the role that Mr Dick is to play in the novel to justify Betsey's claims about him.

GLOSSARY   *Chapter 41*
            tucker lady's soft cloth or scarf tucked over the bosom

CHAPTERS 43–45

David's marriage

David established in his career.

At 21, David has mastered shorthand and earns a good income from reporting debates in Parliament for a morning paper. He has become an author as well and makes a very good living by his writing. Traddles has tried, without success, to be a reporter and has now been called to the bar.

The Misses Spenlow have consented to the marriage of Dora and David and are fussing about the preparations. Sophy and Agnes are to be bridesmaids.

In true Dickens fashion, Sophy turns out to be all that is wonderful and Agnes gets on very well with Traddles. In the vestry after the wedding, Dora becomes hysterical, crying for her dear father. David and Dora are happy together but their servant, Mary Anne Paragon, turns out to be a disaster. The young couple have their first quarrel about the housekeeping and Dora resorts to tears to get her own way. Her reaction is very similar to that of Clara when arguing with Peggotty.

Servants take advantage of their naivety.

Aunt Betsey wisely declines to mediate between Dora and David. The young couple make up their differences and Mary Anne is sacked. They have a succession of equally unsatisfactory servants and discover that everybody they deal with cheats them. The house is completely disorganised and uncomfortable.

Traddles comes to dinner, which is a failure. Dora begins to see her deficiencies, but still wants to be treated as a child. David feels the need for more depth in her, so that she might be a support to him. By now, his writings have made him famous and Dora wants to feel part of his success, so that, out of kindness, David pretends he needs her to copy his writing. She continues to play at housekeeping to little practical effect.

Dr Strong feels he is a hindrance to his wife, because of their discrepancy in age, and Mrs Markleham encourages this, in order to go on outings with her daughter. She hurts the Doctor by referring to the differences in age and outlook between Annie and himself.

Mr Dick determines to heal the rift between Dr Strong and Annie. He feels he can do what others cannot in this situation.

Mr Dick's plan

Betsey and David, some weeks later, visit the Strongs, when Mrs Markleham bustles in, all of a fluster. She has, by accident, discovered Dr Strong in the study making his will and overheard that he is leaving all he has, unconditionally, to Annie as a mark of his confidence in her. Mr Dick takes Annie into the Doctor's study and lays his hand on the Doctor's arm in a symbolic gesture.

PART 4: THE RISE AND FALL OF HEEP

Annie kneels at her husband's feet and gazes into his face. She appeals for someone to come forward to explain the shadow which has come between herself and her husband. David reveals Heep's insinuation that Annie and Maldon have been having an affair. Annie declares that, from her childhood, she has been attached to Dr Strong who was her tutor. She grew up admiring him and married him for love, not gain.

Annie's protestation of love.

Mrs Markleham has hurt Annie in the past, by suggesting that the marriage will profit her financially. Annie has been upset, and so has Mr Wickfield, by the many demands made by Mrs Markleham upon Dr Strong, for the benefit of her family. There has been no affair with Maldon, with whom Annie has nothing in common. She realised that Mr Wickfield has suspected her of infidelity on the night Maldon went to India.

What had disturbed Annie that night was the discovery of Maldon's ingratitude and falseness. She has lived under these suspicions ever since, yet has never been unfaithful. David reflects on his own marriage, in the light of what Annie said – 'no disparity in marriage like unsuitability of mind and purpose' (Chapter 45, p. 610).

COMMENT

David is no longer poor and can afford to marry Dora. They seem not in the least bit suited, but David is madly in love and forgives everything. Their home is in chaos and Dora cannot cope. It is touching to see her need to be part of David's success and the way he helps her to feel she is.

Mrs Markleham proves the cause of much suffering within the Strongs' marriage. Annie's resolution of her marriage problems is one of the dramatic highlights of the novel. It has been the role of Mr Dick to bring about the reconciliation.

GLOSSARY

Chapter 44

capers pickled flower-buds of a Sicilian shrub

CHAPTERS 46–48

The search for In passing Steerforth's house, David is invited to come
Emily   in and speak to Miss Dartle. She informs him that
                 Emily has left Steerforth, and summons Littimer to
                 give the details. After extended travel on the Continent
                 Steerforth grew restless as Emily became moody and
                 depressed. He proposed to marry her off to Littimer.
                 Emily reacted violently to this infamous proposal and
                 had to be forcibly restrained. She escaped from her
                 locked room and has disappeared. As a consequence,
                 Littimer was dismissed by Steerforth and returned
                 home. He admits having previously intercepted mail to
                 Emily from home. David threatens Littimer that he
                 will let Mr Peggotty know of his part in the story. Rosa
                 Dartle's bitterness against Emily knows no bounds; she
                 blames Emily, not Steerforth, for it all. Mrs Steerforth
                 is a shadow of her former self and, like Rosa, she also
                 blames Emily rather than her son.

                 Mr Peggotty is still scouring London for Emily.
                 He keeps his lodgings in good order, in expectation
                 that she will be found. He is certain that she is still
                 alive.

Martha's role in   David believes that Martha will know if Emily ever
the novel.   returns to London. He and Mr Peggotty find Martha
                     and follow her home at a discreet distance.

Martha's   The area where she lives is squalid and the river there
degradation.   polluted. Her tone of voice expresses her despair and
                 she seems suicidal. Mr Peggotty is much moved by her
                 plight and wonders whether Emily is in a similar state.
                 Martha assures David that she played no part in
                 Emily's elopement and she protests her love for her. Mr
                 Peggotty does not stand in judgement upon Martha for
                 having fallen so low; Emily's fate has changed his
                 attitude to fallen women.

PART 4: THE RISE AND FALL OF HEEP

Martha responds to Mr Peggotty's appeal for help to find Emily. She refuses to give her own address and will not accept any money, seeing it as her duty to help Emily. She now has the complete trust of Mr Peggotty and David.

On returning to Highgate, by his aunt's cottage David again sees the strange man he had seen with her in London. He is after money, but Betsey cannot give him enough. He refuses to leave and seems to have some hold over her.

Betsey confesses to David that the man is her husband, who has drained her of money and sunk very low in life; still she cannot dismiss him from her life. She wants this to be a secret between her and David.

David's marriage not entirely happy. David's success as a novelist now allows him to give up reporting on Parliament. He and Dora have continuous trouble with dishonest and incompetent servants.

In vain does David try to make Dora face the fact of her hopelessly deficient housekeeping; she stops him by using emotional blackmail. He tries to educate her, by talking learnedly to Traddles, hoping Dora will listen intently, but this, too, is a failure. He wants Dora to be his soul-mate, but has to admit that there is a gulf between them and he gives up trying to improve her mind.

Though he loves Dora, thoughts of Agnes come into his mind and he feels that he will never again find the contentment he found in her company. If his heart had been more disciplined, he might not have married Dora.

The maturity that motherhood brings is not to be for Dora; she miscarries and her health deteriorates. David is stricken with grief about her ill-health and fears the worst.

COMMENT   In the exchanges between Rosa Dartle, Littimer and David, Rosa's cruelty and spite become plain. Littimer will disclose confidences to those by whom he is employed, but not to others. Money is the arbiter of his morality.

Up to now, Martha has just flitted in and out of the story, but she has an important part to play in the efforts to find Emily.

Dora refuses to grow up and insists on her childish ways. The loss of her unborn child has a serious effect on her and on the outcome of the novel.

GLOSSARY   *Chapter 46*
fleet shallow

CHAPTERS 49–53

Mr Micawber's promise of revelations

Mr Micawber writes to ask David to meet him at the King's Bench Prison and David believes that he has something serious on his mind. Traddles has a letter from Mrs Micawber, worried at the change she sees in her husband, which she thinks is the consequence of a mental disturbance. She knows he is going to London, but does not know why. She wants Traddles to see him and act as an intermediary between him and his family.

Traddles and David meet Micawber who is a changed man. He evidently has Uriah Heep on his mind. The villainy of Heep is preying on him. He is in a fever of anxiety and is intent on destroying Heep; he grows hysterical and rushes off. Almost at once a letter is received from him, confirming an arrangement to meet them all, David, Traddles, Betsey and Mr Dick, in Canterbury.

David fears that Emily is dead, but Mr Peggotty still clings to hope. He has received a cryptic message from Martha, warning him not to leave London.

Martha is the key to Emily's salvation.

Near his cottage, David discerns Martha beckoning to him. She has news for Mr Peggotty, but has not found him at home and has left a message. They take a coach into London and Martha leads David into a house in the slums, teeming with people. A female figure is fleetingly seen entering Martha's room, as they are ascending the stairs. Though unknown to Martha, she is recognised by David as Rosa Dartle.

Rosa seen in all her viciousness.

They listen at the door to Rosa's taunting insults, delivered with a vicious cruelty. Emily tries to escape, but she is stopped by Rosa, who is gloating over her plight and expressing her contempt for Emily's family. Emily defends them though not herself. Rosa threatens to proclaim Emily's story wherever Emily goes. On hearing Mr Peggotty's footsteps, Rosa leaves and Emily swoons into his arms.

Mr Peggotty's plan.

The following day Mr Peggotty tells Emily's story to Aunt Betsey. He tells of the kindness shown by a friendly woman in Italy. Emily then journeyed through France, where she found work, until Littimer came there and she fled to England. Martha has been looking after her in London. Betsey is overcome by this account and is in tears.

Mr Peggotty plans to emigrate to Australia with Emily, but first he intends to return to Steerforth the money given to Emily. He wishes David to accompany him on his farewell visit to Ham and Peggotty.

Ham blames himself for Emily's behaviour.

Peggotty now lives at Ham's house. She, Ham and Mrs Gummidge have been told the whole story and both women are in tears. Ham wants Emily to forgive him for putting pressure on her to marry him. He still loves her and is heartbroken, but wants to put her mind at rest about him. Mrs Gummidge begs to go along with Mr Peggotty and Emily to Australia, and this is agreed. Dora is unwell, but insists that Betsey go with Mr

Dick, Traddles and David to see Mr Micawber in Canterbury. They find Mr Micawber behaving very oddly. He takes his leave of them, requesting they should follow him five minutes later.

Mr Micawber drops the bombshell

Consequently, Betsey, David and Traddles and Mr Dick follow him to Mr Wickfield's house, where Mr Micawber greets them as though he had not met them earlier. Heep is taken by surprise, but is as fawning as ever. Mr Micawber brings in Agnes; her father, being unwell, is not able to be present. Uriah tells Mr Micawber to go, but he defies the command, upsetting Heep greatly. Mr Micawber now confronts Heep with his wickedness. Uriah realises he is trapped, suspects David of having hatched a plot against him and lets his mask of humility slip. He threatens Betsey and Agnes and shows that he despises everyone, but his main venom is directed at David.

Mr Micawber produces a letter, in which he charges Heep with trapping him into poverty, with bullying Mr Wickfield into signing illegal documents, and with forgery. Micawber possesses a book, in which Heep has practised forging Mr Wickfield's signature. Traddles has earlier taken possession of the firm's books, and now he demands that Heep pay back all the stolen

PART 4: THE RISE AND FALL OF HEEP

money (including Aunt Betsey's) and keep to his room or be gaoled. Heep capitulates, but holds David responsible for his downfall.

Emigration as a solution for the Micawbers.

Mr Micawber is now reconciled to his wife and family and there is a happy reunion. Aunt Betsey suggests that the Micawbers should emigrate and offers to finance the venture.

Dora's death

Dora, now very ill, thinks back to her early married days and would like to recapture them. She asks to see Agnes and shows more concern for David than for herself; she feels now she will never recover. David has been told that Dora is dying but he cannot comprehend it. Dora is resigned to her fate and thinks it best for David. Agnes is with Dora as she dies.

COMMENT

The tide is now turning for the better as Martha and Mr Micawber begin to act. Rosa is seen in her true colours. Mr Peggotty and Ham are shown as noble characters, caring only for others and never for themselves.

The sinister plotting of Uriah Heep is exposed, in a scene of great dramatic power. He will not regain his power to work evil again.

Emigration is seen as the solution for Emily, Mr Peggotty, Martha and the Micawbers, giving them all the chance of making a new and freer life for themselves.

David's good angel, Agnes, consoles the dying Dora who makes a strange request of her of which we learn later.

GLOSSARY

Chapter 49
Immortal exciseman Robert Burns

Chapter 51
Sermuchser so much so

A *Identify the speaker.*

1 'The circumstances that distressed me are not changed, since I came into this room; but an influence comes over me in that short minute that alters me, oh, how much for the better!'

7 "Tis more as I beg of her to fogive me, for having pressed my affections upon her'

6 'There can be no disparity in marriage like unsuitability of mind and purpose'

2 'She clenched both her hands; shut her eyes; turned lead-colour; became perfectly stiff; and took nothing for two days, but toast and water'

5 'If she hadn't stood my friend, sir, I should have been shut up, to lead a dismal life these many years'

3 'He never could come into the office, without ordering me ... about. One of your fine gentlemen he was!'

4 'If you meant to reason with such a poor little thing as I am, you ought to have told me so, you cruel boy!'

Think about the circumstances in which these words are said and what they tell us of the character of the speakers or of their subjects.

Check your answers on page 96.

B *Consider these issues.*

a Dickens's criticism of court practices.

b The scene in which Mr Wickfield cries out against Heep.

c The scene in which Heep informs Dr Strong that Annie is having an affair.

d Mr Dick's role in the reconciliation of the Strongs.

e The married life of Dora and David.

f Annie's protestation of love for Dr Strong.

g Rosa's hatred of Emily and the reason for it.

h Martha's role in the story.

i Mr Micawber's accusations against Heep.

PART 5: HAPPY ENDINGS

CHAPTERS 54–57

*Death of
Steerforth; the
emigrants
depart*

*Mr Dick makes
himself useful.*

Agnes is a great support to David in his sad loss. He
has decided to seek solace in travelling abroad.

Something is troubling Aunt Betsey, but she will not
confide what it is. Mr Dick has been guarding Heep,
and he has also been most helpful in clerical matters.
Mr Wickfield is making a good recovery, and it is
found that he is not bankrupt after all. Traddles has
recovered Betsey's money stolen by Heep in order to
deprive David of an inheritance and financial support.
The money having been recovered, Heep and his
mother are allowed to depart for London.

*The death of
Betsey's husband.*

What has been worrying Aunt Betsey, it is disclosed, is
the death of her husband, whose funeral she and David
attend.

David writes to Emily about Ham and wants to take
her reply directly to him and bring back Ham's reply to
her, before she sails. A great storm of unprecedented
ferocity arises, so that the coach and horses have a
struggle to reach Yarmouth.

*Another
coincidence used to
dramatic effect.*

David is roused from slumber by calls about a wreck
nearby which is breaking up. Ham determines to reach
the wreck to which one man alone is still clinging.
Ham, on the point of reaching the ship, is swallowed
up along with the ship by a mountainous wave, and
pulled back to dry land, dead. Another body is
recovered also – that of Steerforth, whom Ham was
attempting to save.

*Rosa embittered
and vindictive.*

David goes to Mrs Steerforth with the news of her
son's death. Rosa attacks Mrs Steerforth accusing her of
having caused her son's death. She is in a frenzy and
has no regard for Mrs Steerforth's agony.

Mr Micawber is asked to prevent news of the tragedy reaching Emily or Mr Peggotty. He has been repeatedly arrested on a writ from Heep, and released upon David's payment of his debt.

Emigration as a solution to many problems.

The emigrants make their farewells and the ship leaves for Gravesend. Heep has had Mr Micawber arrested on board ship and Mr Peggotty, as arranged by David, had paid the money to rescue him for the last time. On the ship, David repays Mr Peggotty and meets Martha, who is one of the party bound for Australia.

COMMENT

Aunt Betsey tends to keep her own problems to herself, not to burden others with them. She retains some affection for her wayward husband to the very last. She had only pretended to have taken her financial affairs into her own hands and failed in order to shield Mr Wickfield. In reality, Heep stole her money.

Traddles is the saviour in the end and the one who defeats Heep's evil aims, with Mr Micawber's evidence.

The great storm and the deaths of Ham and Steerforth are a dramatic highlight of the story.

Dickens appears to look upon emigration to Australia as an answer to the social ills affecting the poor.

GLOSSARY

Chapter 54
incubus oppressive evil spirit

CHAPTERS 58–60

David's return to England

David is in a deep depression because of his loss of Dora and his depression does not lift during his travels abroad. Only Agnes's reassuring letters give him hope for the future and he begins to write again.

Traddles is happily married.

His thoughts dwell on Agnes, and he feels that he has thrown away any hope of her love. After three years, he

PART 5: HAPPY ENDINGS

returns to England. He finds Traddles is happily married and doing well. David meets Sophy along with her sisters on his visit to Traddles. They are all devoted to one another.

All seem content now but David.

David has news of Mr Murdstone, who has remarried and is subjecting his second wife to the same harsh treatment as the first, always using religion as a cloak for his cruelty.

The news from Australia is good: the emigrants are all doing well, and Mr Micawber is repaying his debts, bit by bit.

At home, Mr Dick is happily working for Traddles, and Mr Wickfield, now old, is contented.

David considers proposing marriage to Agnes.

David asks his aunt, who is full of praise for Agnes, whether Agnes has a lover, only to receive a cryptic answer. She knows, in her heart, that Agnes loves David, but she will not reveal it outright. At last, David realises he is in love with Agnes. Yet he is afraid to propose to her as he feels he may be rejected and their closeness destroyed.

Visiting the Wickfields in Canterbury David confesses to Agnes that he owes her a great debt, but he still delays his proposal.

COMMENT

David's absence from England does not prevent Agnes from giving him comfort through her letters. Traddles has promised to look after Sophy's family, should the need arise, and has overcome all obstacles to his marriage; even the emigrants are happy with their lot. David alone is discontented. Agnes enjoys running her little school, but there is still 'the same sad smile' (Chapter 60, p. 772) to be seen on her face on occasions, which betrays a lack of complete fulfilment.

GLOSSARY   *Chapter 59*
                Britannia metal an alloy of tin, antimony, copper and lead
                pounce fine pumice powder dusted over paper to make a better
                    writing or drawing surface
                negus mixture of wine and hot water sweetened and spiced

CHAPTERS 61–64

David   David is living at Betsey's, while writing his next book.
marries Agnes He is famous now and some people wish to use his
                name for their shady Doctors' Commons practices, but
                he will not allow it. He receives a letter from Creakle,
                now a magistrate, in which he offers to show him the
                only way to convert villains, that is, by solitary
                confinement. He has become tenderhearted, but only to
                prisoners.

                David and Traddles take up his offer and David
                considers, when he sees the prison, that more money is
                being spent on prisons than on educating the young or
                caring for the old.

David meets Heep   The two model prisoners are Uriah Heep, in prison for
and Littimer in   forgery and fraud, and Littimer, arrested with the help
prison.   of Miss Mowcher and sentenced for theft. The prison
                     visitors are entirely taken in by these two pious frauds,

PART 5: HAPPY ENDINGS

but the warders are not. Both Traddles and David despise Mr Creakle's prison system.

Convention did not allow women to take the lead.

David resolves to propose to Agnes. He asks her if she has a lover and Agnes becomes very upset; but when he tells her that he loves her she replies that she has loved him all her life.

Betsey's delight at this news knows no bounds. Within a fortnight, David and Agnes are married.

Good news from Australia

They have been married ten years, when Peggotty returns from Australia, bringing good news about all the emigrants. Mr Micawber has paid all his debts, has worked hard, is now a magistrate and writes articles for a local newspaper. Mr Peggotty returns to Australia, and they will never see him again.

Julia Mills returns from India with her grumpy, but rich Scottish husband. She has become completely mercenary. The sneering Maldon is part of the same set and David finds these people repugnant. Dr Strong is never going to finish his dictionary and Traddles ends up accommodating Sophy's sisters in his grand house.

David lives in peaceful contentment with his beloved Agnes.

COMMENT   The **theme** (see Literary Terms) of corrupt justice is touched upon at two points here: the use of famous names to obtain business in Doctors' Commons and the way in which magistrates were chosen. Dickens disapproves also of the large amount of money spent on model prisons, while the education of the young and the care of the old are neglected.

David has learned now not to be deceived by the hypocrisy of Heep and Littimer, whereas Creakle, full of self-importance, thinks he is doing a wonderful job reforming villains.

The strict conventions of etiquette have been remarked upon before and here they are shown to be so strongly instilled in Agnes that she risks losing all rather than break them. David has never treated Agnes like the other women he has met, but now he has matured, realising that emotion previously blinded him to the truth.

Many saw Australia as the promised land of opportunity, as does Dickens here. In *David Copperfield* people don't take their problems with them when they emigrate as they do in real life.

A final comment on society is to be found in Julia's pursuit of riches as her sole object in life and Maldon's continuing sneers at goodness.

GLOSSARY   Croesus fabulously rich king of Lydia

A *Identify the speaker.*

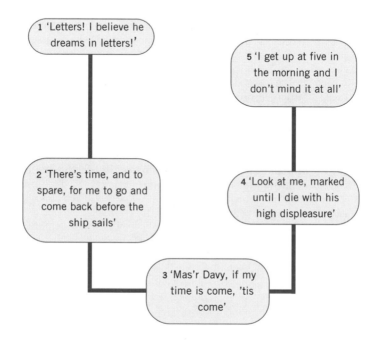

1 'Letters! I believe he dreams in letters!'

5 'I get up at five in the morning and I don't mind it at all'

2 'There's time, and to spare, for me to go and come back before the ship sails'

4 'Look at me, marked until I die with his high displeasure'

3 'Mas'r Davy, if my time is come, 'tis come'

Think about the circumstances in which these words are said and what they tell us of the characters of the speakers.

Check your answers on page 96.

B *Consider these issues.*

a The role of Mr Dick in the story.

b Rosa's attitude to Mrs Steerforth.

c Agnes's continuing concern for David.

d The etiquette of the times.

e The corrupt practices in the judicial system.

f The mature attitude of David towards Agnes compared to his earlier attitude to women.

PART THREE

COMMENTARY

THEMES

DAVID'S JOURNEY TO MATURITY

The main **theme** (see Literary Terms) of the novel is David's development to maturity in his perception of the world and in his emotional life. The hardships suffered at home under the Murdstones, at Salem House, in Murdstone and Grinby's warehouse and on the road to Betsey's may not help his emotional development, but they certainly open his eyes to the harshness of a world where the strong prey upon the weak. At Betsey's and at Dr Strong's school, where kindness and affection are evident, David is able to develop those skills necessary to cope in the world, whereas under Murdstone and Creakle he was too terrified to make any progress. Later, thanks to his talent and earnest hard work, he achieves financial and literary success.

Despite being offended by Heep's repulsiveness, David fails to recognise his essential wickedness and allows himself to be used against Dr Strong. He sees the real Uriah Heep only when the mask is torn aside by Mr Micawber's accusations. Steerforth's charm and good looks hide from David the reality of his character, even after the Mr Mell episode. It is only when Steerforth elopes with Emily that David realises what his true character is. Later, it is very noticeable that he is not deceived by the 'model' prisoners, Heep and Littimer, as Creakle and the prison visitors are.

David's emotional life is under the sway of any young lady he happens to meet – Miss Shepherd, Miss Larkins, Dora – making him quite oblivious of the realities of the situation. It is only at the end, when he

recognises Agnes as his soul-mate, that he has fully
matured emotionally.

EXPLOITATION OF THE POOR AND WEAK

Early on, we have an example of the Victorian husband
in Mr Murdstone, abusing his power over his wife,
Clara, and his stepson, David, and repeating the process
later with a new wife.

The same abuse of power, on a large scale, was to be
found in too many schools. Before 1870, there was no
national system of accountability in education, and
Creakle's school, being free from government
interference, may not be far removed from some actual
schools at the time. Child labour under harsh
conditions is criticised in the episode at Murdstone and
Grinby's warehouse: an experience similar to one
Dickens himself endured, and a common practice in
those days.

Children (the weak) are given no protection from adults
(the strong), just as, on the coach journey to London,
the adults have no consideration for David and make
his journey most uncomfortable. The waiter at the
inn (Chapter 5, pp. 71–3) exploits his innocence and
youth, as does the 'long-legged young man' (Chapter
12, pp. 172–3) who steals his money and belongings.
Even the poor exploit the poor on David's journey to
Aunt Betsey's.

Those who are made vulnerable by poverty are
victimised, as we can see from the Micawber family's
being imprisoned for debt, as Dickens's own family
was. Unable to pay their bills, Mr Micawber and his
family are ejected from their home and have all their
goods confiscated. Even their lodger, Traddles, suffers
the same fate.

Mr Wickfield's weakness for drink allows his exploitation by Heep, and Emily's pretensions to be a lady are exploited by Steerforth for his own ends, as he has always exploited David's innocence.

Dr Strong is another innocent, taken advantage of by many, but particularly by Maldon, Mrs Markleham and Uriah Heep; the latter also forces Mr Micawber to accept terms of employment favourable to himself.

LOVE CONQUERS ALL

Most of the characters who suffer in the novel, are rescued by the loving care and consideration of others. This is why we are left with a happy feeling at the end, despite the tragedies that occurred.

David is rescued from the Murdstones' neglect by Aunt Betsey, from ignorance by Dr Strong and from mental turmoil by Agnes. Mr Micawber is saved from his life of penury by Betsey's loan which enables him to emigrate to Australia. Mr Wickfield's rescuers are Mr Micawber and Traddles, who also save Betsey from poverty. Mr Dick restores the marriage of the Strongs to its former harmony, while he himself has been saved from the asylum by Betsey.

Finally, Mr Peggotty is responsible for enabling Emily, Martha and Mrs Gummidge to live decent lives in Australia.

On balance, we can justly claim victory for good over evil.

THE JUDICIAL SYSTEM

The judicial system is condemned by Dickens every time it is touched upon. Steerforth tells us about the lawyers' monopoly in law suits and wills, marriages and shipping disputes, and what a cosy, profitable affair it all is. We learn with David that advocates and proctors have a snug little business going between them, without outside interference.

When David visits Spenlow and Jorkins, he uses religious language (temple, pilgrims) to describe the hallowed atmosphere (Chapter 23, p. 327). It is an institution frozen in time. Mr Spenlow's very clothing is a **symbol** (see Literary Terms) of the stiffness and inflexibility of the system. His hypocrisy, in putting the blame for unpopular decisions on Jorkins, seems to be common practice in the profession, employed in the pursuit of gain. David finds Doctors' Commons like a family party, comfortable and unruffled.

Mr Spenlow, as a representative of the institution, opposes all David's ideas for a fairer system. In Mr Spenlow's opinion, it is ungentlemanly to try to improve anything. He thinks that to interfere with these 'hallowed' institutions will bring the country down. He approves of the exploitation, just as he himself exploits the name of Jorkins to deny Peggotty any reduction of fees.

The way Creakle has become a magistrate is also criticised by Dickens. It is suggested he might have been given the office because he has done someone a favour, or perhaps because he knows somebody who has recommended him to the lieutenant of the county for nomination.

The only lawyer to behave honourably is Traddles, but he looks grave when he thinks, mistakenly, that David is asking him what he thinks of the system (Chapter 61, p. 779).

The novel was produced in a serial form, consisting of twenty parts. Each serialised section ends with an episode designed to encourage the reader to buy the next instalment. Interest is maintained by this device throughout what is a long story. The division of the novel into twenty sections is given in Appendix B on pages 814–855 of your edition.

The novel is written in the form of an autobiography, with the mature David looking back over his past life. David's life is therefore the main unifying factor, but unity is also achieved by the reappearance, often by the use of coincidences, of characters introduced earlier in the novel. The lives of the characters are so threaded together and, mostly, so impinge on David's life, that we see the novel as a whole and not as several parts linked together.

Characters other than David are woven into the story in such a way that they interact with several other characters, not just with David alone, creating a rich tapestry, not a series of loose ends. For instance, the rescue of several people from misery is achieved by Aunt Betsey.

Even the **subplots** (see Literary Terms), like the Strongs' marriage problem and Aunt Betsey's husband's behaviour, are part of David's learning process and do not detract from the unity of the tightly controlled story of David's growth to maturity.

CHARACTERS

DAVID COPPERFIELD

David is an imaginative child, with a romantic bent, as we see from his imagining the pulpit in church as a castle and thinking how he would defend it, as well as from his playing the parts of his heroes and trying to live up to them. He is very observant, too, in his description of Mr Murdstone, for instance. His affectionate character is evident in his innocent love of Emily, when he declares he 'should be reduced to the necessity of killing [himself] with a sword' if she does not love him (Chapter 3, p. 44).

Imaginative
Sensitive
Romantic
Affectionate
Unselfish
Susceptible

He is sensitive and feels very insecure when the Murdstones change the appearance of the house. His timidity prevents his learning his lessons when harassed by the Murdstones, yet he has the spirit to bite Mr Murdstone when beaten by him. His innocence then makes him wonder whether he will be sent to prison; it also makes him a victim of the waiter at the coaching inn and of his fellow travellers. The young David is self-effacing and does not like to admit he is hungry on the journey to Salem House.

His romantic nature makes him an easy tool of Steerforth, whom he sees as a hero. Unselfishly, he forces himself, though weary, to tell his stories to Steerforth at bedtime. He is a self-contained and well-organised boy at the age of ten, fending for himself, while working at Murdstone and Grinby's, and when running away to Aunt Betsey's.

He has a true understanding of his own abilities and has ambitions. Hence, his despair at Murdstone and Grinby's. At Aunt Betsey's, David has the courage to stand up to the Murdstones. His courage is revealed again in his fights with the Canterbury butcher.

His susceptibility to ladies persists from childhood (Emily), through youth (Miss Shepherd, Miss Larkins) to adulthood (Dora). His romantic infatuations make him lose his judgement.

When he leaves school, his romantic view of himself and the world is utterly impractical; the firmness required of him by Betsey does not come to him easily and he is intimidated by the coachdriver and the London waiter.

On meeting Steerforth again, even after learning about the cause of Rosa's scar and hearing Steerforth's scornful, unfeeling remarks about honest people, David in his naivety still sees him as a hero.

David is appreciative of the good he has received in life, which includes for him the friendship of Peggotty and Steerforth. He responds to the kindness of Betsey and Dr Strong. He is sensitive to the feelings of others, not wanting to disclose to anyone Emily's distress. He has a lively social conscience and despises the injustices of the judicial system and the manipulation of the weak by the strong. He is solicitous for Betsey's finances as he tries to recover his fees from Spenlow and Jorkins.

The goodness in him always appreciates the goodness in others (Peggotty, Betsey, Agnes, Ham, Dr Strong, Traddles) and he is very industrious, doing extra work at Dr Strong's to help expenses. He is overwhelmed by the tragedy of others (Ham) and delighted at other people's good fortune (Traddles and Sophy).

He needs the support of a soul-mate ('Deep, downright, faithful earnestness', Aunt Betsey calls it (Chapter 35, p. 466)), which Agnes provides for him throughout, and Dora cannot. His kindness prevents him from blaming Dora for her inadequacies. His patience with Dora (and Jip) borders on perfection.

AUNT BETSEY

Aunt Betsey , a great eccentric, is fundamental to the novel. From her comic behaviour at David's birth to her hysteria at David's engagement to Agnes, she is a prime mover of events. She adopts David, when he has no future, wards off the Murdstones' evil influence, has David educated and sets him up in a career. She is kind-hearted and emotional, but tries to hide her emotions by attributing them to others, for instance, to David's mother (Chapter 19, p. 259).

Eccentric
Affectionate
Generous
Forthright
Outspoken
Independent

It is because of Betsey, that David becomes involved with Mr Wickfield, Agnes, Heep, the Strongs, Mr Dick, Dora and Julia. The story would not exist without her. She not only finances David when he needs it, but also tries to encourage his independence by sending him off to Yarmouth and London on his own, which is the cause of his meeting Steerforth again, with the resultant tragedy to Emily and her consequent emigration with Mr Peggotty, Mrs Gummidge and Martha.

Betsey is very supportive of David, even when he makes the wrong marriage choice. She wisely refuses to intervene, when Dora and David have their differences. Betsey provides the money, not only to keep Mr Micawber out of prison, but also to enable him and his family to emigrate.

She is a larger-than-life character, who suspects that everyone she meets in London is a criminal and that any house she stays in there will be susceptible to spontaneous combustion. She is forthright in her opinions of the Murdstones, Mrs Markleham, Heep and Mrs Crupp; she does not suffer fools gladly and recognises evil where it exists.

Her kindness is evident in her support for Mr Dick and her constant encouragement of him, while she protects him from his own simple, overgenerous nature. The inner sensitivity of her nature is revealed by her inability to reject her feckless husband. She is a very private person, as far as her own feelings are concerned, and it is only on her husband's death that she makes David, and David only, aware of the situation. She openly admits that David has been a good influence on her.

Finally, she steers David towards proposing to Agnes, by telling him that Agnes is to be married. Her dearest wish comes true then, and through her influence David gains lifelong happiness.

MR MICAWBER

Verbose
Great letter-writer
Thriftless
Volatile
Convivial
Family-loving

Mr Micawber is one of Dickens's great comic creations. At his first meeting with the ten-year-old David, Micawber overwhelms him with his circumlocutions, a trait, which is to become his trade mark. He is forever in debt and harassed by creditors, to the point where he is threatening to commit suicide one minute, but resiliently humming a tune the next. Both he and his wife address David as though he were an adult. He later frequently refers to David as the 'companion of my youth' (Chapter 49, p. 646). Certainly, David receives little fatherly care from Mr Micawber, other than advice on economics ('Annual income twenty pounds, annual expenditure nineteen nineteen six, result happiness' – Chapter 12, p. 170).

The character is based on Dickens's own father: both end up, with their families, imprisoned for debt. Mr Micawber is an emotional man, who is good company, as we see at David's dinner party, before Littimer's appearance. He has the honesty and courage to reveal the wickedness of his employer to his face and, as a consequence, saves Mr Wickfield, Agnes and Aunt Betsey's money, which later enables him to emigrate to a happier life.

His fondness for words extends to prolific letter-writing, so that Aunt Betsey exclaims: 'I believe he dreams in letters!' (Chapter 54, p. 713). His evidence which condemns Heep is also given in a letter. A great deal of **comedy** (see Literary Terms) derives from his verbal overelaboration, both spoken and written, and from his pompous attitude when living in dire poverty.

Unexpectedly, he is happy ('extremely delighted' – Chapter 36, p. 493) to learn of Aunt Betsey's financial misfortune, and, when he is himself solvent, he finds it hard to cope with prosperity. Traddles is certainly used shamelessly by him, but once in Australia, he honours all his debts and finds a vehicle for his verbal extravagance in journalism and in his pronouncements as a magistrate.

URIAH HEEP
Evil
Vengeful
Hypocritical
Repellent
Smarmy
Ambitious

Uriah is, from the start, unattractive in appearance, mannerisms and attitude. David is uncomfortable in his presence. Heep seems unable to smile and is compared to cold-blooded or slimy creatures (fish, snails, eels, snakes); quite strikingly, Dickens expresses Heep's evil nature in visual **images** (see Literary Terms) only. His habitual squirming drives Betsey to distraction ('Don't be galvanic, sir!' – Chapter 35, p. 478).

Uriah sees David as his rival for a partnership with Mr Wickfield and for the hand of Agnes. He preys upon Mr Wickfield's weakness for drink, humiliating him before others and dominating him totally. He defrauds Mr Wickfield and Betsey and casts a shadow over the Wickfield household, controlling even domestic affairs with his mother's help. He is entirely wicked and uses Wickfield and David to attack the Strongs' marriage, because he has an ancient grudge against Maldon and Annie. To achieve his ends, he uses blackmail, spying, forgery and the sowing of suspicions.

When he employs Mr Micawber, he thinks, wrongly, that he can buy his silence, but in the end Mr Micawber exposes him. Heep lets the mask slip and we see him in all his wickedness. His persistent vengeance results in Mr Micawber's frequent arrests for debt before he can finally leave the country.

Heep resumes his fawning mask again while in prison, to deceive the prison visitors. Needless to say, he does not deceive either David or Traddles.

STEERFORTH

Handsome
Talented
Spoiled
Arrogant
Unprincipled
Selfish

Steerforth has no father and is spoiled by his rich mother. He uses his charm to win over the young David and to spend his money for him. His status at Salem House makes him a hero in David's eyes. David is blind to his arrogance and scorn for the poor. Only Traddles objects to his treatment of Mr Mell.

He selfishly makes David tell him stories at night, even when David is tired and sleepy.

When he and David meet again at the hotel, Steerforth receives privileged treatment and is exacting in his demands for service. On seeing David's lodgings his first remark is he will use them as his town house (Chapter 24, p. 334). Though at university, he has no intention of working for a degree and is just pursuing his own pleasures. His remarks about Peggotty's family are most disparaging, especially as they immediately follow David's invitation to visit them. The scar on Rosa's face bears witness to the vicious blow he had dealt her when in a rage as a boy. He admits he is lazy, but does not want to do anything about it.

Though contemptuous of them at heart, Steerforth charms the Peggottys, especially Emily, and his thoughts turn to winning her from Ham. He recognises

David's integrity and his own lack of it; he feels guilty when David praises him.

His philosophy of life is selfishness, but he realises he has never had a worthy cause to pursue. There is **dramatic irony** (see Literary Terms) in Ham's vain sacrifice of his own life in trying to save Steerforth. We may remember here his contemptuous references to Ham as a 'chuckle-headed fellow' (Chapter 21, p. 298), a 'lout' (Chapter 22, p. 301).

AGNES
Good
Full of kindness
Calm
Serene
Steadfast in her love

At their first meeting, David is impressed by Agnes's tranquillity. She appears mature beyond her years. She is her father's reason for living, his constant support and housekeeper. She radiates goodness and peace and will become David's 'good angel', his constant adviser.

Agnes never condemns, not even David's drunkenness at the theatre, but she warns him against Steerforth with some slight success, since David sees her as a paragon. She well understands Heep's tactics and speaks of them to David. Agnes likes to be informed about David's infatuations, because she has always loved him in secret. Her kindliness extends even to the obnoxious Mrs Heep, and Betsey confides in her, young as she is. She exercises a calming influence on David and without her he is lost.

Agnes understands even Dora and advises David sensibly on the right approach to her guardians. Dora on her sick-bed needs Agnes's company. Agnes, alone, is with Dora when she dies and is urged by Dora on her deathbed to marry David. In his sorrow, David receives support from Agnes, even when abroad, but convention does not allow her to disclose her love and David cannot be certain of it.

He recognises that Agnes has the qualities that Dora lacked. When he proposes, she confesses she has always loved him and the novel is brought to a happy end.

Agnes remains the same from beginning to end; she does not develop or change and at times seems more like a benign presence than a real person.

DORA
Pretty
Spoiled
Childish
Affectionate
Perceptive

Dora has beauty but little depth. Though everybody spoils her, she has no self-confidence and is frightened to meet Betsey and later Agnes. She cannot bear to hear her faults mentioned and bursts into tears at the gentlest reproach. She is alarmingly impractical and will not be taught to improve, but goes on behaving like a spoiled child.

She is perceptive enough to wonder why David loves her and not Agnes. Perhaps surprisingly, Agnes has a high opinion of her, and Betsey gets on well with her, too. Dora has an affectionate nature and responds to love and affection. She wants to be treated like a child and cannot face decisions like getting rid of bad servants. She is easily bored by what she finds difficult, but likes to bask in the reflected glory of David's success, by 'helping' him in his work. She is impervious to learning and gets her own way through emotional blackmail, believing: 'It is better for me to be stupid than uncomfortable' (Chapter 48, p. 642). There is something missing in her relationship with David and she is aware of this. She believes that her death will be better for David in the long run. She shows courage and resignation in the face of death and wants Agnes to take her place.

MINOR CHARACTERS

Barkis

Barkis brings some **humour** (see Literary Terms) into the story with his eccentric courtship of Peggotty. His illness delays Ham's marriage to Emily and so contributes to the catastrophe. A simple character, miserly, but devoted to his wife and proud of her.

Mr Chillip	A comic figure, mild and timid, he almost apologises to the newspaper for reading it (Chapter 59, p. 763). A kindly man, perceptive.
Clara Copperfield	She is pretty, rather spoiled and vain, but loves David. Her vanity leads her into a disastrous second marriage. She is easily browbeaten and moulded by the Murdstones.
Creakle	Creakle is a vicious child-beater later transformed into a gullible do-gooder and magistrate. Authoritarian, he rejects his own son for disagreeing with him, and maltreats his wife and daughter.
Mrs Crupp	Mrs Crupp is a comic character, crafty, greedy and lazy. She does not like her lodger to entertain guests, and is routed by Aunt Betsey.
Rosa Dartle	Rosa is consumed by jealousy of Emily, because she wants Steerforth for herself. She is unforgiving, cruel and spiteful.
Mr Dick	Mr Dick is backward, but kindly, surprisingly shrewd in some ways. He heals the rift between the Strongs and gives Betsey an opportunity to show her goodness.
Martha Endell	Martha is a fallen woman, who redeems herself by saving Emily. Her behaviour affects Mr Peggotty's way of judging women of her kind.
Mrs Gummidge	Mrs Gummidge is a sorry creature, wallowing in self-pity until Emily elopes, when she becomes a great support to Mr Peggotty.
Mrs Heep	She is as wicked as her son and helps him in his evil designs. She does love him, repulsive as he is.
Littimer	Steerforth's servant employed by him to engineer Emily's flight from home. A man with no good qualities, he betrays his resentment when Emily refuses to be married off to him by Steerforth. He too is a model prisoner in Mr Creakle's penal institution.

Mrs Markleham	Mrs Markleham abuses Dr Strong's goodness and gullibility. She brings the news of the doctor's will.
Jack Maldon	Maldon is a cynical, unprincipled self-seeker, who despises the unfortunate and battens on Dr Strong.
Mrs Micawber	Mrs Micawber loves her husband and believes in his talents. Like him, she is subject to extremes of emotion, but she is a good wife and mother.
Julia Mills	Julia indulges in **melodrama** (see Literary Terms) and takes herself and her early experience too seriously. She acts as go-between for David and Dora and thoroughly enjoys it. In the end she marries a rich old man and is 'steeped in money to the throat' (Chapter 64, p. 804).
Miss Mowcher	Miss Mowcher is a very colourful character, a cheerful and energetic dwarf who brings **humour** (see Literary Terms) into the story. She tries to prevent the elopement of Steerforth, by whom she has unwittingly been used. She helps to capture Littimer later.

Mr Murdstone

Murdstone is an autocrat, who ill-treats cruelly, and with evident enjoyment, anyone in his power, always under the guise of morality. He hates David and wants him out of the way. His only redeeming feature is that he really loved Clara, though her pretty house and her income probably added to her attractions in his eyes.

He uses his young second wife, a rich heiress, so cruelly that he has crushed her spirit and driven her to the edge of madness. In this he is abetted by his sister, **Jane Murdstone**, a harsh, unfeeling woman with no redeeming qualities.

Peggotty

Peggotty is a loving, kind nurse to David, and more an affectionate friend than a servant to Clara Copperfield. Later she is the kind and understanding wife of Barkis, tolerant of his comic miserliness.

She is hard-working, honest and courageous, and sees through the pretences of the Murdstones.

It is through Peggoty that David meets Dan Peggotty, Emily and Ham, and therefore through Peggotty again the fatal link is made between David's treacherous friend Steerforth and Emily.

Mr Peggotty

Dan Peggotty is Peggotty's brother, a simple, good and kindly man of great moral strength. He has adopted Emily and Ham, the orphaned children of his relations.

The pretty, wilful, spoiled **Emily** is his darling, and his love for her never falters. He forgives her at once for what she has done, and in his untiring search for her he shows nobility of mind and generosity of heart.

There is a silent understanding of two noble minds between him and Ham. **Ham** may be a humble fisherman but in his relationships with David, the innocent cause of so much suffering, and with Emily, he displays delicacy of feeling and moral integrity which show up Steerforth as the coarse-minded, arrogant egotist that he is.

Mr Spenlow

Mr Spenlow is the unbending champion of the status quo as far as the law is concerned. He hypocritically blames his partner for his own acquisitiveness, but he is a loving father, even though he believes money is more important to a marriage than love.

*Mrs
Steerforth*

Mrs Steerforth is proud, even arrogant, and has spoiled her son completely, but she shows kindly concern for David at his loss of Dora. She cannot accept that Emily is good enough for her son.

Dr Strong	Dr Strong is amiable, kind-hearted and easily put upon. He loves his wife dearly, even when he has been falsely told that she has been having an affair. He has been a great teacher and guide for David and employs him as his secretary when David needs the money.
Annie Strong	Annie is a loving wife who is maligned by Heep. Her declaration of love for her husband is very moving.
Traddles	Traddles is a man of complete integrity. As a boy he was the only one to protest against Steerforth's treatment of Mr Mell, and as a man he is a good friend to David, helping him to find a way to earn his living.

He is married to **Sophy**, of whom he always speaks as 'the dearest girl'. She has looked after her mother and sisters all her life, and Traddles cheerfully takes on the burden of assisting his wife's large family. Sophy's sisters all think a great deal of him.

Mr Wickfield   Mr Wickfield is devoted to his daughter, Agnes, but his weakness for wine enables Heep to take over his law practice and embezzle his money. He recovers somewhat after Heep's defeat.

LANGUAGE & STYLE

In *David Copperfield*, Dickens uses the intimate device of **first person narrative** (see Literary Terms), with hesitations and diversions that are decidedly convincing. He stops the narrative from time to time to engage in detailed descriptions in order to impress people and situations on our imagination.

He demonstrates his ability to enter the mind of the innocent young David, who feels sorry for all the imaginary cares of the waiter, who has been taking advantage of him (Chapter 5, p. 73).

A great amount of **humour** (see Literary Terms) is evident in the characterisation of such people as

Mrs Crupp and her 'spazzums' (Chapter 26, p. 359). It is to be found of course in Mr Micawber's pompous language. Humour may be also the vehicle for **irony** (see Literary Terms), as in Betsey's reply to Uriah that he is 'pretty constant to the promise of his youth' (Chapter 52, p. 685) or in David's prison visit.

Dickens shows his awareness of the symbolic value of words in his descriptions. The 'fetters' and 'rivets' worn by Miss Murdstone are effective **symbols** (see Literary Terms) of the barren, unfeeling soul within (Chapter 26, p. 366). Mr Spenlow himself seems a symbol of an inflexible institution from his starched cravat and shirt collar to his 'undeniable boots' (Chapter 23, p. 328). The mist like 'a stormy sea' (Chapter 46, p. 621) rising to the feet of Rosa and Mrs Steerforth, Dora's empty chair (Chapter 53, p. 704) are powerful symbols used with great effect.

Melodrama (see Literary Terms), beloved of the Victorians, is used to what seems to us ludicrous effect in the death of Jip and perhaps more successfully in Martha's self-abasement, though even there it is still excessive to modern taste. The narrative can be very moving (Peggotty's account of Clara's illness and death in Chapter 9; Annie's confession of her love for her husband in Chapter 45) but also sugary sweet at times (the description of Agnes with Dora in Chapter 42).

The **dramatic irony** (see Literary Terms) Dickens employs is understood only after we have read the novel, but it shows the care that has been used in its construction: 'the brightest night of [Mr Peggotty's] life as ever was or will be' (Chapter 21, p. 293) is the night Steerforth arrives.

The overwhelming power of Dickens's writing, however, lies in the magnificence of the characters he creates.

PART FOUR

STUDY SKILLS

HOW TO USE QUOTATIONS

One of the secrets of success in writing essays is the way you use quotations. There are five basic principles:

- Put inverted commas at the beginning and end of the quotation
- Write the quotation exactly as it appears in the original
- Do not use a quotation that repeats what you have just written
- Use the quotation so that it fits into your sentence
- Keep the quotation as short as possible

Quotations should be used to develop the line of thought in your essays.

Your comment should not duplicate what is in your quotation. For example:

> **David looks back at Mrs Steerforth and Rosa and sees that 'the mist [is] rising like a sea, which ... made it seem as if the gathering waters would encompass them'.**

Far more effective is to write:

> **David looks back at Mrs Steerforth and Rosa and thinks that the rising mist looks like a rising sea, and that it seems as if 'the gathering waters would encompass them'.**

However, the most sophisticated way of using the writer's words is to embed them into your sentence:

> **As David looks back at Mrs Steerforth and Rosa, it seems to him that the mist rising from the valley surrounds the two women like 'the gathering waters' of the sea.**

When you use quotations in this way, you are demonstrating the ability to use text as evidence to support your ideas - not simply including words from the original to prove you have read it.

Everyone writes differently. Work through the suggestions given here and adapt the advice to suit your own style and interests. This will improve your essay-writing skills and allow your personal voice to emerge.

The following points indicate in ascending order the skills of essay writing:

- Picking out one or two facts about the story and adding the odd detail
- Writing about the text by retelling the story
- Retelling the story and adding a quotation here and there
- Organising an answer which explains what is happening in the text and giving quotations to support what you write

....

- Writing in such a way as to show that you have thought about the intentions of the writer of the text and that you understand the techniques used
- Writing at some length, giving your viewpoint on the text and commenting by picking out details to support your views
- Looking at the text as a work of art, demonstrating clear critical judgement and explaining to the reader of your essay how the enjoyment of the text is assisted by literary devices, linguistic effects and psychological insights; showing how the text relates to the time when it was written

The dotted line above represents the division between lower and higher level grades. Higher-level performance begins when you start to consider your response as a reader of the text. The highest level is reached when you offer an enthusiastic personal response and show how this piece of literature is a product of its time.

Coursework essay

Set aside an hour or so at the start of your work to plan what you have to do.

- List all the points you feel are needed to cover the task. Collect page references of information and quotations that will support what you have to say. A helpful tool is the highlighter pen: this saves painstaking copying and enables you to target precisely what you want to use.
- Focus on what you consider to be the main points of the essay. Try to sum up your argument in a single sentence, which could be the closing sentence of your essay. Depending on the essay title, it could be a statement about a character: From their first meeting, Steerforth has used David for his own ends quite unscrupulously; an opinion about setting: Mr Peggotty's boat was a cosy home, fitting for the homely family, but it carried an association with the sea that was to bring them tragedy; or a judgement on a theme: Annie's words on 'the unsuitability of mind and purpose' sum up the reason for David's awareness of something missing in his marriage to Dora.
- Make a short essay plan. Use the first paragraph to introduce the argument you wish to make. In the following paragraphs develop this argument with details, examples and other possible points of view. Sum up your argument in the last paragraph. Check you have answered the question.
- Write the essay, remembering all the time the central point you are making.
- On completion, go back over what you have written to eliminate careless errors and improve expression. Read it aloud to yourself, or, if you are feeling more confident, to a relative or friend.

If you can, try to type your essay using a word processor. This will allow you to correct and improve your writing without spoiling its appearance.

Examination essay

The essay written in an examination often carries more marks than the coursework essay even though it is written under considerable time pressure.

In the revision period build up notes on various aspects of the text you are using. Fortunately, in acquiring this set of York Notes on *David Copperfield*, you have made a prudent beginning! York Notes are set out to give you vital information and help you to construct your personal overview of the text.

Make notes with appropriate quotations about the key issues of the set text. Go into the examination knowing your text and having a clear set of opinions about it.

In the examination

In most English Literature examinations you can take in copies of your set books. This in an enormous advantage although it may lull you into a false sense of security. Beware! There is simply not enough time in an examination to read the book from scratch.

- Read the question paper carefully and remind yourself what you have to do.
- Look at the questions on your set texts to select the one that most interests you and mentally work out the points you wish to stress.
- Remind yourself of the time available and how you are going to use it.
- Briefly map out a short plan in note form that will keep your writing on track and illustrate the key argument you want to make.
- Then set about writing it.
- When you have finished, check through to eliminate errors.

To summarise, these are keys to success

- Know the text
- Have a clear understanding of and opinions on the storyline, characters, setting, themes and writer's concerns
- Select the right material
- Plan and write a clear response, continually bearing the question in mind

SAMPLE ESSAY PLAN

How important is letter writing in the development of the story?

Letters play an important part in the novel.

Part 1   Peggotty's letter tells David where Aunt Betsey lives.

Part 2   Through finding Aunt Betsey, David:
- receives a good education
- meets the Wickfields, Heep and Mr Spenlow
- becomes a proctor and meets Dora

Part 3   Mr Micawber's letter accusing Heep results in:
- the destruction of Heep
- the saving of Mr Wickfield
- the restoring of Betsey's wealth
- the Micawbers' emigration with Betsey's help

Part 4   Agnes's letters to David when abroad:
- console him in his loss and give him hope
- make him realise what he has apparently lost in not marrying Agnes

Part 5   Emily's letter to Ham causes David to revisit Yarmouth where he witnesses:
- Ham's bravery and death
- Steerforth's death

Conclusion   If these letters had not been written, other devices would have been necessary for the story to continue as it does.

Make a plan as shown above, and attempt to answer the following questions:

1 Which parts of the novel moved you most and why? Limit yourself to four examples and discuss them with close reference to the text.

2 What part do hypocrisy and deception play in the story? How do they add to the reader's enjoyment?

3 What sorts of comments does Dickens make in this novel about the society of his time? (You need to look at such things as the treatment of children, the judicial system, education, prisons and the treatment of the poor.)

4 Show the importance of Agnes in David's development. Refer closely to the text in your answer.

5 Letters play a significant part in the development of the story. Choose four examples and show their importance to the novel.

6 What part does coincidence play in the story? Confine your answer to six examples and discuss each separately and in detail.

7 This novel is a mixture of the unreal and the realistic. Say where you find each of these attributes and pay close attention to the text in your answer.

8 This novel was written as a serial. What devices does Dickens use to maintain tension and hold the interest of the reader?

9 Give your opinion of Dickens's attitude to women, with reference to Agnes, Dora, Aunt Betsey, Peggotty and Emily.

10 What parallels do you notice between the life of David and the life of Dickens? Discuss three of these parallels and say whether or not the author is successful in making the situations convincing.

CULTURAL CONNECTIONS

BROADER PERSPECTIVES

Films

David O. Selznick's 1934 film of *David Copperfield* (directed by George Cukor) has been highly praised. It is available on video also. David Lean's films *Oliver Twist* (1948) and *Great Expectations* (1946) are both worth seeing.

Other books

Jane Eyre (Charlotte Brontë) again features an orphan cruelly treated and sent to a harsh institution to endure appalling hardships.

Bleak House (Charles Dickens) exposes the corruption at the Court of Chancery where delays and costs consume people's money.

Death of a Naturalist (Seamus Heaney) gives a close description of a child's view of his surroundings.

Mid-term Break (Seamus Heaney) tells of the author's being called home from boarding school for the funeral of his little brother.

Tom Brown's Schooldays (Thomas Hughes) shows us the conditions in public schools.

Portrait of the Artist as a Young Man (James Joyce) where we are given an example of brutal punishment in a school of a different era.

Hard Cash (Charles Reade) is an attack upon the abuses of lunatic asylums.

For the nineteenth-century background of Dickens's novels you might find Norman Lowe's *Mastering Modern British History* (Macmillan Master Series, 1988) both interesting and useful.

LITERARY TERMS

comedy used generally of an amusing story with a happy ending

dramatic irony a development of the plot which will have tragic consequences, which are not foreseen by the characters in the story

first person narrative story told in the first person (an 'I' figure is the narrator who is directly involved in the events of the story)

humour method of description or narration intended to make the readers laugh

image words referring to objects and qualities which appeal to the emotions and the senses

irony saying one thing while meaning another, usually quite the opposite, often with a satirical intention

melodrama writing which refers for effect on sensational events, improbable happenings and violent action, often with sentimental overtones

plot the plan of a novel (or play), an arrangement of the events described which suggests a meaningful pattern of relationships between these events

subplot a secondary plot running parallel with the main plot of a novel. Several subplots may be found in Dickens's novels

symbol something used in writing to represent something else (often an abstract idea)

theme the central idea of a novel; several themes might be identified in the same novel

TEST ANSWERS

TEST YOURSELF (Chapters 1–18)
A 1 Aunt Betsey *(Chapter 1)*
... 2 Mr Murdstone *(Chapter 4)*
3 Mr Creakle *(Chapter 6)*
4 Uriah Heep *(Chapter 17)*

TEST YOURSELF (Chapters 19–30)
A 1 Aunt Betsey *(Chapter 19)*
... 2 Steerforth *(Chapter 20)*
3 Miss Mowcher *(Chapter 22)*
4 Agnes *(Chapter 25)*
5 Miss Murdstone *(Chapter 26)*
6 Traddles *(Chapter 27)*
7 David *(Chapter 28)*

TEST YOURSELF (Chapters 31–38)
A 1 Ham *(Chapter 31)*
... 2 Rosa Dartle *(Chapter 32)*
3 Dora *(Chapter 33)*

4 Traddles *(Chapter 34)*
5 Agnes *(Chapter 35)*
6 Maldon *(Chapter 36)*

TEST YOURSELF (Chapters 39–53)
A 1 David *(Chapter 39)*
... 2 Traddles *(Chapter 41)*
3 Heep *(Chapter 42)*
4 Dora *(Chapter 44)*
5 Mr Dick *(Chapter 45)*
6 Annie *(Chapter 45)*
7 Ham *(Chapter 51)*

TEST YOURSELF (Chapters 54–64)
A 1 Aunt Betsey *(Chapter 54)*
... 2 David *(Chapter 55)*
3 Ham *(Chapter 55)*
4 Rosa Dartle *(Chapter 56)*
5 Traddles *(Chapter 59)*